PHILOSOPHY OF THE BUDDHA

PHILOSOPHY OF THE BUDDHA

A. J. BAHM

PROFESSOR OF PHILOSOPHY
UNIVERSITY OF NEW MEXICO, ALBUQUERQUE

Capricorn Books
G. P. Putnam's Sons
New York

TO
LUNA

'How visioned is the man-of-calm declared,
How virtuous? Tell me, O Gotama,
When asked, the best of men!' The Master said:

'Who conquers craving ere he crumble up,
Who trusts not first things nor the last, nor counts
The middle things: he hath no preference.

Gone wrath, gone fear, gone boasting, gone remorse,
Sooth-speaking, mild: that sage doth curb his talk.

Hoping for naught to come, he mourns no past;
Seer of th' aloof 'mid touch, views lead him not.

Guileless, apart, not fond nor envious,
Not loth nor forward, not to slander giv'n;

Not fain for pleasures nor to pride inclined,
Gentle yet quick, no dupe, dispassionate;

He traineth not in hope of gain, nor moved
Is he at getting none; no craving stirs
His placidness; he hankers not for tastes.

Poised, e'er alert, he deems not in the world
Things "equal", "notable", nor "lacking worth".
For him there are no thoughts of "prominence".

Who trusteth not, knows not a thing on trust,
Thirsts not about becoming or decay.

I call him man-of-calm; not heeding lusts,
Without a knot, he hath the foul mire crossed.

No sons, kine, fields, nor property are his;
Naught to assume or to reject he finds.

Between folk's words, or brahman or recluse,
No choice hath he, hence talk doth move him not.

Gone envy, greed, the sage speaks not of "high",
"Low", "equal", seeking not time's web, weaves none.

Who here hath not, nor grieves o'er loss, nor goes
To views, he truly man-of-calm is called.'

Woven Cadences of Early Buddhists (Sutta
Nipata), pp. 126–7 Tr. E. M. Hare, Oxford
University Press, London, 1945, 1947.

CONTENTS

PREFACE

Gotama, The Buddha, is one of the world's most influential thinkers. What he taught has been interpreted and reinterpreted many times. That he is widely misunderstood is obvious to every scholar, especially to those Buddhists who differ with each other regarding his teachings. The problem, 'What did he really believe?', which interests so many, has intrigued the writer especially as a responsible teacher of comparative philosophies. The need for clearer understanding of the real, and humanly significant, roots, and permanent values of many aspects of Buddhist thought, grows as the peoples of the world become more interdependent.

Everyone is a Buddhist! At least this startling conclusion was forced upon the writer as a result of his studies in the Sutta and Vinaya Pitakas, the two earliest collections of Buddhist records. This assertion does not claim that all subscribe to everything called Buddhist, but only that the teachings of Gotama contain principles which everyone accepts, once he stops to think about them. The purpose of this book is to state the philosophy of Gotama, the man himself, by means of quotations from the Pitakas themselves. This book does not concern itself with the various other Buddhist philosophies constituting the long, devious, profound, and fascinating history of Buddhism, except to challenge their conclusions as attributable to Gotama. It aims also to stimulate further study of the ancient Pitakas by minds uncommitted to traditional interpretations.

The study resulting in this book had many origins. Opportunity for pursuing it was made possible by joint receipt of a grant as Fulbright Research Scholar in Buddhist Philosophy in the University of Rangoon and sabbatical leave as Professor of Philosophy in the University of New Mexico. The writer's long-standing interest in comparative philosophy, expressed recently through nine years of teaching courses in oriental philosophy, generated deepening respect for Buddhist philosophies. Apparent inconsistencies pervading interpretations of what otherwise seemed an intuitively obvious doctrine, aroused growing suspicion that those interpretations which appear artificial or unintelligible were not authentic. Efforts to expound Buddhist ideals sympathetically yielded coherent wholes of valuable insight which, when not completely corroborated by available literature, led to the belief that there must be more vitality, genuine humanity, and universality in the original insights than are disclosed in some accounts.

These doubts were then stimulated by Mohan Singh and supported by Howard J. Parsons. Singh's *New Light on Buddha's First Sermon* (a paper read at the All-India Oriental Conference, Bombay, and published by the Academy of Spiritual Culture, Elephanta, Dera Dun, 1949) presented results of digging about in Sanskrit evidence and maintained, for example, that 'By the rendition of *Arya* as noble, *dukha* as suffering, *sam* as right, the grandest sublimest transcendental teachings of the *Abhisambuddha* have been made un-Arya-like; active *Dhyani* Buddhism has been reduced to stoical pessimistic ethics; and the path of transcendence of the pairs of opposites, expounded in the Gita under *Buddhiyoga*, the path of balance has been made to lose

itself in the medieval forests of rightness and virtuousness.'
(P. 8.) Parson's article, 'Buddha and Buddhism: A New
Appraisal' (*Philosophy East and West*, Vol. I, No. 3,
October, 1951, pp. 8–37), claimed that 'His "middle way"
escapes the painful and uncertainly oscillating dualisms of
his times: the Absolutistic Brahmins and the annihilationists; being and non-being; the desire for existence and the
desire for non-existence; the universal principle (*Brahman*)
and the individual principle (*atman*); the self and the non-
self; permanence and impermanence; theism and atheism;
the world's eternality and the world's temporality; immortality and mortality; life and death; the identity of body and
soul, the separation of body and soul. The directing control
of the ego is the middle way between the expansive and
contracting tendencies of life, between indulgence and
mortification. Gotama follows the middle course through
these dualisms, by not responding to either extreme. . . .'
(P. 18.)

Interest in Gotama's philosophy was sustained by continuing curiosity concerning in how far the writer's own
philosophy, 'Organicism' (Cf. his *Philosophy, An Introduc-
tion*, Ch. 20. John Wiley and Sons, N.Y., 1953), which also
idealizes a middle way as central to philosophy, has ante-
cedents in Buddhism.

The sources used in pursuing the study itself, in the
University of Rangoon from July, 1955, to March, 1956,
consisted primarily in twenty-six volumes of the Vinaya
and Sutta Pitakas in English translations, supplemented by
portions of seventeen volumes of secondary materials (*see*
Bibliography).

Numerous persons and institutions contributed to success of the study. Acknowledgement of indebtedness is due
(1) the United States Educational Foundation in Burma,

especially U Cho, its Executive Officer, and U Htun Myaing, its Administrative Assistant, for their part in providing comfortable and convenient living and study accommodations in Rangoon, (2) the University of Rangoon, especially Dr. Hla Bu, Head of the Department of Philosophy and Psychology, and U Aung Than, Head of the Department of Pali and Abhidhamma, for permission to study in their Departments, (3) Professors K. N. Kar, U Pe Maung Tin, and R. P. Chaudhuri for their critical examination of the completed manuscript, (4) Dr. Devaprasad Guha, Daw Khin Win Kyi, U Tin Lwin, U Lay Myint, and David Maurice for assistance in obtaining books and references used in research, and (5) U Thittila for instruction in the concurrently studied contrasting Abhidhamma (Theravada) philosophy.

Indebtedness is expressed also to I. B. Horner, Honorary Secretary of the Pali Text Society, for detailed critical suggestions regarding the manuscript, to the Pali Text Society, the Oxford University Press, and Luzac and Co., Ltd., for permission to use extensive quotations from their publications, to the other publishers granting permission to quote, and to my wife for many valuable improvements in the manuscript.

PHILOSOPHY OF THE BUDDHA

GOTAMA'S PHILOSOPHY

GOTAMA'S philosophy may be summed up in a simple, clear and obvious principle, which immediately compels belief once it is understood. The principle: Desire for what will not be attained ends in frustration; therefore, to avoid frustration, avoid desiring what will not be attained.

Although immediately obvious, the principle entails certain practical difficulties. First, it is natural to want more —at least a little more—than one gets. The frustration entailed in this unattained more is ever-present. Hence, 'all is suffering'. Secondly, one cannot always anticipate precisely what will be attained. When uncertain regarding the alternative, more or less, one prefers and hopes for the better, the more desirable; but to the extent that this more desirable is more than will be attained, frustration is in prospect. When, further, discomfort regarding uncertainty of predictions arouses interest in improving one's predictive ability, this too adds to frustration to the extent that one then desires to achieve more such ability than he will attain. Thirdly, since effort of will or strength of desire itself often influences the outcome, one ought to desire strongly enough to assure adequate effort; yet since desires do not come with their intensities fitted with automatic stopping devices correlated with what is actually attainable, it is to be expected that desires commonly overshoot their mark.

These practical difficulties do not invalidate the principle. They merely indicate its universality, the subtlety with which it operates, the reason why it is commonly neglected, and need for special effort to bring it into effective operation. The principle explains unhappiness as universal, present in all times and places, because inherent in the nature of desiring. It works subtly, not merely because desires are emotively imprecise, but especially because the desire to prevent desiring more than will be attained is itself unconsciously desired too much. The principle is neglected, not wilfully, but unwittingly, first because people mistakenly search for the causes of unhappiness in the objects of desires, and then, when desire itself is discovered to be the culprit, because the locus of its application undergoes a sleight-of-hand shift, so that whenever a person tackles the problem in one place, it reappears, unawares, in another. Hence this ever-slippery problem requires special effort—a persistent alertness to its perpetual recurrence at each dialectically deeper level of desiring. For whenever one desires to stop 'desiring more than will be attained', this additional, deeper desire also becomes a desire for more stopping than will be attained. Thus this additional, deeper desire requires its own additional, still deeper desire to stop desiring more stopping than will be attained. The problem of unhappiness is an ever-deepening one which can be grasped and solved only dialectically. (Those for whom dialectic is beyond comprehension, hence mysterious, may find here evidence of miraculousness which then blooms as a belief in divinity.) But, as we shall see, dialectical problems solve themselves, if only we will let them. One who finally gives up trying to solve the problem of frustration, thereby becoming willing to accept his desires and frustrations for what they are, finds the problem solved.

The goal of life is neither more favourable rebirth nor extinction of self or of desire, as some have maintained, but 'dwelling, here and now, beyond appetites, consummate, unfevered, in bliss, in (wholesomeness)'. (*Further Dialogues of the Buddha*, Vol. I, p. 247. Tr. Lord Chalmers, Oxford University Press, London, 1926.) Then '. . . to whatever place you go, you shall go in comfort; wherever you stand, you shall stand in comfort; wherever you sit, you shall sit in comfort; and wherever you make your bed, you shall lie down in comfort.' (*The Book of the Gradual Sayings*, Vol. IV, p. 200. Tr. E. M. Hare, Luzac and Co., Ltd., London, 1955.)

How the foregoing succinct summary expresses Gotama's philosophy will become clear only through a review of his own personal struggle, near-defeat, and final victory. Gotama arrived at his conclusion, not by a few moments of reflection, but the hard way: first by staking his kingdom (he was a prince due to inherit his father's realm) and his life (he almost died from starvation after seven years of ascetic practices) in earnest experiments to find life's goal. Abundant pleasures of the princely life he knew first hand. But no matter how lavishly he was supplied, he always wished for more than could be had. Finally, when about thirty years of age, he listened to the counsel of the wise men of his time: the root of life's troubles lies not in insufficiency of objects desired but in desiring. Surrendering his royal robes for ascetic rags and his palace for a begging bowl, he went in search of *nirvana*, the peace that knows no frustration. Trances, mortification, fasts, and the like, although pursued diligently under able teachers, brought him nowhere. Hence he learned that not only did excessive desire end in defeat, but excessive desire for freedom from desire also ended in frustration. His discovery of this fact, while sitting under a tree recuperating from exhausting fasts, constituted his 'Enlightenment', and from it stems his epithet, 'The Buddha', and the name of the long history of interpretations, 'Buddhism'.

His historical (sixth century B.C.) insight, that happiness can be found only in the middle way, appears to agree with other (mostly later) Golden Mean philosophies in advising avoidance of extremes. The awesome example of Gotama's own struggle, first against princely dissipation and then against asceticism, may easily be interpreted as setting the stage for a plea to avoid the extremes of debauchery and mortification. And, since his way is universal, one is tempted to list all pairs of opposites and advise wariness of each extreme and conformity to each mean. However, Gotama's insight focused upon one kind of mean, one which, if achieved, would automatically resolve the difficulties relative to all other pairs of extremes: his middle way is a way between desiring too much and desiring too much stopping of such desiring.

This way involves a double willingness. In order to avoid frustration, one must desire to stop desiring what will not be attained. But to stop desiring what will not be attained requires a desire to stop such desiring. In so far as this additional desire is also a desire for what will not be attained, it, too, ends in frustration. Hence, to stop this additional frustration, one must stop desiring more stopping of desire than will be attained. Here a predicament arises. In seeking to avoid frustration, one finds that he must be willing to be frustrated as much as he will be frustrated; and also be willing to be frustrated relative to his desire to stop desiring as he will be frustrated. This double willingness is the middle way.

The middle way turns out to be the way things are (i.e.,

in all tenses of 'are'), for it is the way between wanting things (including desires) to be more than they are or less than they are with respect to any way that they are. So long as one considers 'seek the middle way' and 'accept things as they are' as two different principles, he has not yet found the middle way. But despite the subtlety required for comprehension and skill demanded for deliberate achievement, the principle, that happiness is to be found in accepting things as they are, is very simple, even if dialectical. Only when one no longer struggles with the problem of frustration does it cease to be a problem; or only when one is willing to be as unhappy as he is can he be as happy as he can be.

If, as the writer contends, Gotama's philosophy consists in a single psychological principle, what about the numerous claims that he held such-and-such views relative to various metaphysical problems? Regarding each question put to him, he replied, typically, as follows. Is there, for example, a next life? That, he would say, is not an important issue. Consider the possibilities: If you desire a next life and there is a next life, you have no problem. If you desire a next life and there is no next life, you will be frustrated. If you desire no next life and there is no next life, you have no problem. If you desire no next life and there is a next life, you will be frustrated. In either case, whether there is or is not a next life, you will be frustrated if you want what will not be. Hence, so far as happiness is concerned, the important issue is not whether there is or is not a next life, but whether or not you are willing to accept things as they will be, however they will be.

To all such questions as 'Is there a soul?', 'Is the soul the same as the body or different?' he gave the same kind of answer: 'That, Potthapada, is a matter on which I have expressed no opinion.' 'But why . . .?' 'This question is not calculated to profit, is not concerned with the *dhamma*, it does not redound even to the elements of right conduct, nor to detachment, nor to purification from lusts, nor to quietude, nor to tranquillization of heart, nor to real knowledge, nor to insight, nor to *nirvana*. Therefore is it that I express no opinion upon it.' 'Then what is it that the Exalted One *has* determined?' 'I have expounded what pain (i.e., unhappiness, frustration, or anxiety) is; . . . the origin of pain; . . . the cessation of pain; . . . what is the method by which one may reach the cessation of pain?' 'And why . . .?' 'Because that . . . is calculated to profit. . . .' (*Dialogues of the Buddha*, Part I, pp. 254-5. Tr. T. W. Rhys Davids, Oxford University Press, London, 1899, 1923.)

Here we have a statement of the 'Four Truths' which are not four principles, but merely one principle, with four statements asserted about it. The principle: desire for what will not be attained ends in frustration; therefore to avoid frustration, avoid desiring what will not be attained. The four statements: (1) Unhappiness consists in frustration (dissatisfaction, anxiety). (2) It originates in desiring what will not be attained. (3) It ceases when one ceases to desire what will not be attained. (4) The method is to seek the middle way between wanting things to be more than they are or less than they are with respect to any way that they are. If this be Gotama's doctrine, surely we are all followers of Gotama, assenting to the truth of his principle, even if, unhappily, we fail to practise it to perfection.

Unfortunately for doctrinal simplicity, the 'Four Truths' have received other formulations, even in the Pitakas themselves. Consider the now-common formula: 'All is suffering, because all is impermanent. The cause of suffering is desire. The way to remove suffering is to remove desire. The way to remove desire is to follow the Eight-Fold Path.'

Although it is clear that Gotama intended his principle to be a universal solution to a universal problem ('All is suffering' meaning that people normally always desire more than they will attain, at least in some degree), the explanation, 'because all is impermanent', appears to be the work of other minds. The importance of the role which this doctrine has played in Buddhist history does not permit it to be lightly cast aside. Yet certain persisting inconsistencies continue to call for more suitable explanation. If all is impermanent, is impermanence impermanent, is the doctrine of impermanence impermanent, is *dhamma* (Gotama's doctrine) impermanent? If attachment to the permanent is evil, should one seek permanent non-attachment? If self is impermanent, what is it that reaps karmic rewards, that is reborn, that continues through the eight steps, through the *ihanas*, or in *nirvana*?

Such inconsistencies disappear when the doctrine of impermanence is treated as an example of 'greed for views' (*see* Ch. 9), and subordinated to Gotama's principle of the middle way: desire neither more permanence nor impermanence than you are going to get. Gotama's view is not that all is suffering because all is impermanent. Rather it is that all is suffering (i.e., all are frustrated because they desire more than will be attained), and this holds true regardless of whether all is permanent, all is impermanent, or both, or neither. Although the doctrine of impermanence, together with the no-soul doctrine, is profusely expressed in the Pitakas, especially in the third or Abhidhamma Pitaka, and accepted as orthodox by Theravadins, it not only is inconsistent with Gotama's central principle but is explicitly denied in other quotations from Gotama. His answer to the question 'Is all impermanent?' is the same as to the question 'Is the world eternal (permanent)?' cited above. To it he would give no definite answer because doing so would be not only seeking, but claiming to have achieved, more certainty than could be attained. Hence the commonly-accepted statement of the first of the 'Four Truths' was rejected by Gotama, not in the sense that he claims that all, or anything, is permanent, but in the sense that he refused to assert either that anything is or is not impermanent.

Did Gotama deny the existence of the metaphysical? No. 'These things do exist and there are those who can see them; and consequently he would be wrong in saying they were non-existent merely because he could not see them.' (*Further Dialogues of the Buddha*, Vol. II, p. 115. Tr. Lord Chalmers, Oxford University Press, London, 1927.) Did he deny that metaphysical problems could ever be solved? No. To deny the possibility of solution would itself involve drawing inferences about the metaphysical and desiring more certainty regarding the truth of such denial than can reasonably be attained. Did he himself discuss such metaphysical problems? Yes, for when such problems were presented to him by people in anguish about them, he sometimes tried to relieve their anguish by examining the problems with them, partly to gain their confidence that he had a sympathetic grasp of their predicament and partly as a means of showing that their trouble lay really not in having failed to settle a metaphysical puzzle but in having failed to realize that over-desirousness must yield frustration in this area also.

Dogmatists, men 'fixed in their theories' (*Woven Cadences of Early Buddhists*, p. 130. Tr. E. M. Hare, Oxford University Press, London, 1945, 1947), and those who would be dogmatists, as evidenced by the tenacity of their search, are possessed of 'greed for views'. To the extent that anyone, in the absence of evidence, is dogmatic, his claiming to have attained more certainty than has actually been attained is an invitation to anguish. Even the desire for more certainty than will be attained, by one who does not yet claim to have attained, is also conducive to anguish. Thus whoever would avoid such anguish must remain in doubt. He must be a sceptic. Only by being sceptical regarding solution to problems which he will not solve (or to the extent that he will not solve them), will one be freed from anguish. However, if the avid seeker, accepting this advice to doubt, then doubts with equal avidity, he becomes, in turn, a dogmatic sceptic, 'doubt completely', or an agnostic, 'no solution is possible'. Going from one extreme to the other, from dogmatism to agnosticism, he has then to be recautioned about agnosticism as greed for no view. Since agnosticism is itself a view, one can as easily be frustrated by over-zealous attachment to it as to its opposite. The middle way, believing neither that one will attain more certainty than he will attain nor that he will attain less certainty than he will attain, again needs to be sought. But again too avid seeking for the middle way embodies a more subtle greed which must be rooted out by more subtle efforts, without pursuing such uprooting greedily, but my means of a still more subtle middle way. The problem of stopping anguish is sufficiently difficult, complex, and attention-demanding that anyone who pursues it with diligence will have little time left over for indulging unhappily in metaphysical pursuits.

The second and third of the 'Four Truths' also tend to be misinterpreted when stated as: 'The cause of suffering is desire, and the way to remove suffering is to remove desire.' It is true that Gotama located the seat of unhappiness in desire, and it is true that removal of desire removes frustration of desire. But the view that Gotama advocated removal of all desire is false. When one has satisfied desires, because he had desired what he was going to get, no unhappiness, no suffering, no problem, exists. (And Gotama did not seek to make a problem where there is none.) Furthermore, in so far as there is an attainable way out of unhappiness, one should desire and seek that way. Misinterpretation arose, doubtless, because of the subtle difference between desire and desirousness, or between *chanda* (desiring what, and no more than, will be attained) and *tanha* (desiring more than will be attained). It arose also because many of his fellow-wayfarers, already accustomed to thinking of desire as evil and extinction as the goal, were not wholly converted. Some transmitters of his sayings continued to interpret them as more akin to the negativism which he rejected than appears warranted.

The fourth of the 'Four Truths' pertains to the way to end unhappiness—the middle way. Why tradition first added, and then substituted, the 'Eight-Fold Path', summarized as 'right belief, right aspiration, right speech, right action, right living, right effort, right thought, and right concentration', needs to be explained. Despite the fact that the Theravada interpretation of Gotama's teaching given by some of his early followers won out and came to occupy a major place in the Pitakas, enough of Gotama's own view also remains to provide refutation. Although a casual scholar or a believing Theravadin can, by citing the scriptures, easily 'prove' that Gotama was a Theravadin, these same scriptures contain also enough of Gotama's own protests against Theravada as well as other misinterpretations to force the careful scholar to a different conclusion.

Disagreement with those who claim that Theravada,

Sunyavada, Shin, Zen or any other of the varieties of Buddhist philosophy was taught by Gotama himself is not intended to minimize the significance of their own insights into human nature or the importance of their additional contributions to human culture. Each of the Buddhist philosophies has a positive contribution to make. But a more careful examination of the evidence should convince us that Gotama's philosophy, although it inspired them and receives partial expression through them, is still different from any of them.

In what follows, we shall turn first to the problem of misunderstanding and to Gotama's complaints about being misunderstood (Ch. 2), then to an exposition of his philosophy and reasons why it came to be subordinated (Chs. 3–11), and finally to some criticisms (Ch. 12).

2

MISUNDERSTANDINGS

THAT Gotama was misunderstood should be clear to every-one. But the ways in which he was misunderstood, the magnitude of such misunderstanding, and the significance of such misunderstanding in contributing to the long history of doctrines mistakenly attributed to him, and the depth and complicatedness of the problem of extricating ourselves, even partially, from further misunderstanding today, are far from clear. The purpose of examining such misunder-standing here is to show that any interpretation of Gotama's philosophy must retain an element of doubt, and that some criterion other than literal interpretation is required in any attempt to reformulate it. The Pali texts exist, but they embody such a profusion of contradictions that the problem of seeking a criterion faces even one who limits himself to the texts alone. Since many spirits were at work behind the letters of the texts, the scholar must decide whether Gotama himself was a confused thinker (yet remaining quite con-sistent in his types of confusion) or select some one of the views expressed in the texts, or even, as some Mahayanists have done, not in the texts, as his own. Since misunder-standings in and of the texts make inference necessary, some readers will wish to consider them. Others may proceed directly to the exposition beginning in Chapter 3.

The present chapter is so arranged as to treat the various

types of misunderstanding as due to: (1) failure of communication generally, (2) lack of comprehension by those who
heard him, (3) difficulties of memorizers, (4) later inventors,
(5) compilers, and (6) inferences of later thinkers. Mistakes
due to translation and historical changes in language, and
the attribution of miraculous power and wisdom by worshippers,[1] are omitted as too obvious for discussion here.

Failure in communication generally is a fact bemoaned
by writers, celebrated and forgotten, from Lao Tzu to
Bergson, or from Socrates to the semanticists, which every-
one surely has experienced for himself. Indeed, it is quite
central to the nature of the philosophical enterprise to seek
to discover not only the nature of reality and of knowledge
but to grasp what is ultimate regarding the ability and in-
ability of men to understand each other. Gotama did not
wholly understand reality, and it may be something to his
credit, not that he did not try, but that he recognized, after
trying, that expecting more understanding than we will get
leads to unhappiness. (*See* Ch. 9.) Likewise regarding communication, Gotama is reported to have felt his enlightenment so incommunicable that he required three urgings by
Brahma Sahampati before he became willing to try: 'This
too were a difficult matter to see, that is to say the calming
of all habitual tendencies, the renunciation of all attachment,
the destruction of craving, dispassion, stopping, *nirvana*.
And so if I were to teach *dhamma* and others were not to

[1] 'We must admit, however reluctantly, that the masses of Asia, who have
seen in the Buddha the Light of the World, have not done so because of his
rationalist doctrines, his chain of causation, which they have understood as
little as we do, or even his wise advice to still passion. They have adored him,
because they have regarded him as the God of Gods, and believed that by
devotion to him they shall attain eternal salvation, consisting of perpetual
bliss. . . . the simple humanity of the wise teacher has been overlaid by a
divinity not his own, one moreover which on his own theory he would have
treated as absurd.' A. Berriedale Keith, *Buddhist Philosophy in India and Ceylon*,
pp. 14–15. Oxford University Press, London, 1923.

understand me, this would be a weariness to me, this would be a vexation to me.' (*The Book of the Discipline*, Part IV, p. 7. Tr. I. B. Horner, Luzac and Co., Ltd., London, 1951.) 'Thinking of useless fatigue, I have not preached, Brahma, the sublime and excellent *dhamma* to men.' (*Ibid.*, p. 9.)

Gotama is reported to have stated the proverbial parable of the blind men and the elephant as evidence of his concern about the general tendency to disagreement. Once a king commanded all who had been born blind to be brought together to examine an elephant. 'To one man he presented the head of the elephant, to another its ear, to another a tusk, to another the trunk, the foot, back, tail and tuft of the tail.' Consequently descriptions varied. 'Those who had been presented with the head answered, 'An elephant is like a pot.' And those who had felt an ear only replied, 'An elephant is like a winnowing-basket.' Those who had been presented with a tusk said it was a ploughshare. Those who knew only the trunk said it was a plough; they said the body was a granary; the foot, a pillar; the back, a mortar; the tail, a pestle; the tuft of the tail, just a besom. Then they began to quarrel, shouting: 'Yes, it is!' 'No, it is not!' (*The Minor Anthologies of the Pali Canon*, Vol. II, pp. 82, 83. Tr. F. L. Woodward, Oxford University Press, London, 1935, 1948.)

Lack of comprehension by those who heard him is evidenced profusely:

(1) Apparently he made too many converts too quickly, reported as a thousand in a single day (*see* account of the conversion of the Kassapa brothers and their followers. *The Book of the Discipline*, Part IV, pp. 32–44), to have made clear to all of them, or even more than a few of them, the import of his teaching. Conversion must have meant only a willingness to hear him further or a consent to become his

pupil, as even today wearers of yellow robes enter the ranks as probationary novices. His followers were seekers, not necessarily understanders, of his insights.

(2) The congregations of mendicants surrounding Gotama were, both early and late, more fellowships of seekers than disciplined bodies of converts to a rigid doctrine. Hence they were under no pressure to understand him precisely. At times there was considerable doubt as to whether he or other mendicants among his supposed converts were leaders: 'Then it occurred to those . . . brahmans and householders: "Now, does the great recluse (Gotama) fare the Brahma-faring under Kassapa of Uruvela or does Kassapa of Uruvela fare the Brahma-faring under the great recluse?"' (*The Book of the Discipline*, Part IV, p. 47.)

(3) His disciples did not always even pretend to understand him, as in the case of Assaji, one of the first disciples, who replied to the inquiring Sariputta: 'I indeed, friend, am new, not long gone forth, fresh to this *dhamma* and discipline. I am not able to teach you *dhamma* in full, but I will tell you its purport briefly.' (*The Book of the Discipline*, Vol. IV, p. 53.) The record says that 'a number of highly distinguished young' monks requested: 'All our ideas are derived from the Lord, guided by Him and fortified by Him. We pray that the Lord may be pleased to explain what He has said.' (*Further Dialogues of the Buddha*, Vol. I, p. 330.) Sometimes disciples, after hearing Gotama, went away and asked other advanced disciples the meaning of what he had said; the record testifies again and again to their failure to understand. (Cf. *Middle Length Sayings*, Vol. I, pp. 141–8. Tr. I. B. Horner, Luzac and Co., Ltd., London, 1954.)

(4) Even Gotama was aware that sometimes his universal doctrine was mistaken as having merely particular import: 'Now I am aware that when I am teaching *dhamma* to

companies consisting of many hundreds, each person thinks thus about me: "The recluse Gotama is teaching *dhamma* especially for me." But this should not be understood thus. For when a Tathagata is teaching *dhamma* to others it is for the sake of general instruction.' (*Middle Length Sayings*, Vol. I, p. 303.)

(5) On the other hand, often when he addressed himself to the problems of specific individuals in particular situations, listeners interpreted his sayings as universal commands (e.g., as regards many rules for monks).

(6) He spoke in similes, and apparently called up a rich variety of figures to drive home his central point: 'Sense-pleasures are likened by me to a skeleton . . . to a lump of meat . . . to a torch of dry grass . . . to a pit of glowing embers . . . to a dream . . . to something borrowed . . . to the fruits of a tree . . . to a slaughter-house . . . to an impaling stake.' (*Middle Length Sayings*, Vol. I, p. 170.) Such a plethora of examples must have confounded the duller wits who were so overwhelmed by the task of remembering not wholly clear figurative examples that the main general principle escaped them. The remembered examples then served as a basis upon which later scholars speculatively generalized new principles or new versions of the old principle.

(7) At other times, when he used traditional language to express a new idea, the familiar traditional language stuck in the minds of his hearers, with the old rather than the new idea attached to them. 'The Buddha could not disregard the ordinary terminology of his time; his teaching had to be expressed in the terms of his day, and accommodated for practical purposes to ordinary intelligence; the new wine had to be poured into old bottles.' (A. Berriedale Keith, *Buddhist Philosophy in India and Ceylon*, p. 14.) As the new

wine itself became old, it became increasingly difficult to distinguish between the ageing wine and the aged bottles.

(8) Disputes among his hearers arose repeatedly. Occasionally he cried out about misrepresentation: 'There are some recluses and brahmans who misrepresent me untruly, vainly, falsely, not in accordance with fact, saying: "The recluse Gotama is a nihilist, he lays down the cutting off, the destruction, the disappearance of existent entity." But this, monks, is just what I am not, this is just what I do not say, therefore these worthy recluses and brahmans misrepresent me untruly. . . .' (*Middle Length Sayings*, Vol. I, p. 180.) He begged: 'In case you do not understand the meaning of what I have said, I should be questioned about it by you.' (*Ibid.*, p. 172.)

(9) Each monk was free to promote his own philosophy or, at least, his own version of it. Except for advising timid novices, the group was not authoritarian, but like a brotherhood of fellow-seekers. Even the monks close to Gotama, when called upon to describe their ideal teacher, expressed divergent preferences. Ananda: 'a monk who has heard much, who masters what he has heard, who stores what he has heard', etc. (*Middle Length Sayings*, Vol. I, pp. 264–5.) Revata: 'a monk who delights in solitary meditation . . . , a cultivator of empty places'. (*Ibid.*, p. 265.) Anuruddha: 'a monk surveys the thousand worlds with purified *deva*-vision surpassing that of men'. (*Ibid.*) Kassapa: a monk who both is himself and praises: forest-dwelling, almsman, rag-robe wearer, few wishes, contented, aloof, ungregarious, of stirred-up energy, moral habit, possesses concentration, possesses intuitive wisdom, freedom, knowledge and vision. (Cf. *ibid.*, p. 266.) Moggallana: 'intelligent conversationalists'. (Cf. *ibid.*, pp. 266–7.) Sariputta: 'a monk has rule over

mind, he is not under mind's rule; whatever attainment of abiding he wishes . . . he attains at will'. (*Ibid.*, p. 267.) How did Gotama's principle fare when filtered through minds of disciples stressing such different ideals?

The record then quotes Gotama, quizzed as to which had spoken best, as saying: 'It was well spoken by all of you in turn. But now hear me. . . .' (*Ibid.*, p. 271.) Then followed a portrayal of his ideal as one persisting in effort until wholly freed from anxiety. Gotama expected a certain amount of disagreement and misunderstanding, and he would have been inconsistent with his principle if he had complained too much about it. His middle way required him not to be attached to either too much or too little communication or to either too much or too little being understood. Each man had his own right to his own ideals and Gotama could hardly object when his own many-sided life was reflected with varying emphases in the ideals of his fellows. Yet, when his ideal became submerged repeatedly, he appears to have been unhappy about it.

Difficulties of memorizers must be added to those of initial comprehension. First, not only were the memories of those who heard him selective, sifting, consciously or unconsciously, those parts of his message which were most suited to their particular needs, curiosity, or pride, but also the language and ideas used to re-express what they remembered were slanted and often distorted in the re-telling. Secondly, difficulties of second-, third- and fourth-hand memorizers, which increasingly remembered words at expense of meanings, centred on mnemonic devices and shortened formulas which had to be refilled to restore the full meaning. The refilling was sometimes partly forgotten and needed to be reconstructed; occasionally a similar-sounding word with a different meaning was drawn out from the memorizer's vague recollection. The powerful part which artificial numbering played in memorizing is to be seen in the superficially organized collections in 'The Book of the Ones', 'The Book of the Twos', 'The Book of the Threes', through the elevens. Sterility of merely formal memory receives rebuke in the record itself: 'Some foolish men master *dhamma*. . . . These, having mastered that *dhamma*, do not test the meaning of these things by intuitive wisdom; and these things whose meaning is untested by intuitive wisdom do not become clear. . . .' (*The Middle Length Sayings*, Vol. I, p. 171.)

Later inventors of stories, finding them more readily heard if attributed to the honoured authority of the Buddha, did so as a deliberate teaching device. Furthermore, many such stories, retold again and again without the names of authors attached, were conveniently assigned *en masse* to Gotama who, having then come to be considered omniscient, obviously must have known about them anyway. Confusion existed due to the fact that many different names attributed to Gotama, such as 'the Exalted One', 'Tathagata', 'Bhagavan', 'Samana', and 'Buddha', were common general names applied also to other respected teachers. Gotama's disciples were also exalted and enlightened, especially those who survived him and replaced him as effective teachers, as they should have been if they in fact embodied his *dhamma* in their lives. Each *arahant*, achieving *nirvana*, achieves enlightenment, or becomes a Buddha; his teaching, then, comes on a par with that of Gotama; what harm can there be in confusing all such messages from exalted ones when, after all, they are essentially the same?[2] Evidence abounds that the same teaching was attributed to many

---

[2] This line of thought eventually appealed more to Mahayanists than to Hinayanists.

different specifically-named individuals and conflicting teachings were sometimes attributed to the same author. Not only the dialogues and other sayings in the Sutta Pitaka but also the Jataka tales illustrate this tendency. (*See* Maurice Winternitz, *A History of Indian Literature*, Vol. II, pp. 113–56. University of Calcutta, 1933. *See* also C. A. F. Rhys Davids, *The Book of the Gradual Sayings*, Vol. III, p. vi.)

Compilers, faced with the unenviable and overwhelming task of making sense of and finding order in the unmanageable bulk of stories, are to be commended for keeping them together at all. It is indeed amazing to all who think about it that such a mass of materials, partly reinterpreted through variant dialects, should have survived through oral tradition and palm-leaf notation until finally chiselled in stone—this latter being no small achievement in itself. How far the result was a compromise of two conflicting philosophies, democratic inclusion of all extant and available versions versus deliberate selection of those preferred, can only be guessed.

As an example of the compilers' handiwork, consider the following lengthy reference to excerpts from two chapters, consisting respectively of ten and eleven sections, each devoted to a different answer to the same or similar questions concerning what six things are required for living 'happily here and now, neither vexed, troubled, nor fretful; and, on the breaking up of the body after death, a well-faring may be expected?'

Chapter VIII. Section 1: 'Brooding on sense-desires, ill-will, cruelty; and conjuring up like thoughts.'

Section 2: 'Conceit, underrating, overrating, complacency, stubbornness and instability.'

Section 3: 'Forgetfulness in mindfulness, lack of self-possession, unguardedness as to the sense-doors, lack of moderation in eating, deceit and mealy-mouthedness.'

Section 4: (Positively stated) 'delights in *Dhamma*, in growth, in renunciation, in solitude, in being free of ill-will and in non-diffuseness.'

Section 5: 'Unskilled in entering, in leaving, in approach, has no wish to attain unattained skill in *Dhamma*, preserves not his skill attained, nor stirs to persevere.'

Section 6: 'Has clear sight in much, application in much, zest in much, dissatisfaction in much, shirks not the burden of right things, and drives across to the beyond.'

Section 7: 'Takes life, takes what is not given, lives carnally, lies, has evil desires and wrong views.'

Section 8: 'Lies, is slanderous, harsh, a babbler, greedy, reckless.'

Section 9: 'Is without faith, modesty or fear of blame, is indolent, lacks insight and hankers after action and life.'

Section 10: 'Desires much, is fretful, discontented with this and that requisite, robe, alms, lodging, medicaments— is without faith or virtue, is indolent, forgetful in mindfulness and lacks insight.'

Chapter IX. Section 1: 'Checks not the mind when it ought to be checked; exerts not the mind when it ought to be exerted; gladdens not the mind when it ought to be gladdened; gives no heed to the mind when it ought to be given heed to; is bent on low things and finds delight in life's bundle.'

Section 2: 'Cumbered by the stop of action, the stop of vice, the stop of (action's) ripening, he is an unbeliever, lacks urge and lacks insight.'

Section 3: '(By him) his mother's life has been taken, his father's, an arahant's, the Tathagata's blood has been drawn intentionally, the Order embroiled, and he is weak in insight, a witless dullard.'

Section 4: 'Has no desire to listen, incline the ear, apply the heart of understanding, when the *Dhamma*-discipline declared by the Tathagata is taught; he grasps the profitless, rejects the profitable and possesses not himself in harmony and patience.'

Section 5: 'The wrong view of life's bundle, doubt, belief in the adequacy of rule and rite, passion, hate, infatuation.' Sections 6 and 7 repeat 5.

Section 8: 'Live without respect, without regard, for the Teacher, *Dhamma*, the Order, the training; . . . will fall back on the view: "Nothing matters", cannot become one who will beget the eighth state of becoming.'

Section 9: 'Cannot . . . accept any phenomenon as permanent, accept any phenomenon as happiness, accept anything as self, do an unpardonable act, fall back on curious ceremonies for purification, seek outside (the Order) for a gift-worthy.'

Section 10: 'Not . . . take his mother's life, his father's, an arahant's, with evil mind draw the blood of the Tathagata, embroil the Order, point to another teacher.'

Section 11: 'Cannot . . . fall back on the view that weal and woe are self-wrought, are wrought by another, are wrought both by oneself and another, arise by chance without act of the self, or of another, or of both the self and another.' (*The Book of the Gradual Sayings*, Vol. III, pp. 301–6. Tr. F. M. Hare, Luzac and Co., Ltd., London, 1934, 1952.)

And what shall we think when compilers include the following earthy eulogy of wealth, property, prosperity, and fame in a collection devoted primarily to cessation of desires, ending of rebirth, and *jhanas*? 'Monks, by increasing ten growths the Ariyan disciple grows in the Ariyan growth, takes hold of the essential, takes hold of the best for his person. What then? He grows in landed property, in wealth and granary, in child and wife, in slaves and folk who work for him, in four-footed beasts; he grows in faith and virtue, in love, generosity and wisdom.' (*The Book of the Gradual Sayings*, Vol. V, pp. 93–4. Tr. F. L. Woodward, Luzac and Co., Ltd., London, 1936, 1955.)

Inferences of later thinkers, coming along after the canon had solidified and responsible for exfoliation of the various schools within Buddhism, contribute their fundamental part to the total picture of misunderstanding of the philosophy of Gotama. They cannot all be correct in attributing their views to Gotama, though anyone learning about Buddhism today is likely to be introduced first to the point of view of some particular school. Gotama's refusal to give serious answer to metaphysical questions and the multitudes of answers to these questions given by Buddhists together constitute Buddhism, for Buddhist philosophy is not a single philosophy but a whole history of philosophies to which the philosophy of Gotama is but a stimulating prelude. All those who have drawn inferences, as I am doing, risk reading into his philosophy much more, or less, than was there. Great ingenuity has been exercised in many of these historical inferences, some of which have merit quite independently of their specific contribution to Buddhism. But wherever inference is involved, caution regarding mis-understanding must be exercised, as the record itself warns: 'Grasping the *dhamma* is like grasping a snake; if you grasp it in the wrong place, it will turn and bite you painfully.' (Cf. *The Middle Length Sayings*, Vol. I, p. 172.)

3

THE FOUR TRUTHS

LIFE's basic problem, why and how to live, is conceived
by Gotama in a common-sense manner. Why live? To
enjoy life: 'seek . . . for the self an abiding ease here and
now.' (*Middle Length Sayings*, Vol. I, p. 30. *See ibid.*, p. 52.)
How live? Freed from frustration: 'having overcome both
hankering and dejection common in the world.' (*Dialogues
of the Buddha*, Part II, p. 101. Tr. T. W. and C. A. F. Rhys
Davids, Luzac and Co., Ltd., London, 1910, 1951.) What
is the means for achieving such freedom? 'And to that I
should reply: "Why this very personality that you see
before you is what I mean."' (*Dialogues of the Buddha*,
Part I, p. 261.) Does this require withdrawal from the
world? No. 'Certain recluses and brahmans have falsely,
emptily, mendaciously and unfairly accused me, saying:
Gotama, the recluse . . . has said: Whenever one has attained
to the stage of deliverance, entitled the Beautiful, one then
considers all things as repulsive. But this, Bhagava, I have
not said. What I do say is this: Whenever one attains to the
stage of deliverance, entitled the Beautiful, one is then
aware " 'Tis lovely."' (*Dialogues of the Buddha*, Part III,
pp. 31–2. Tr. T. W. and C. A. F. Rhys Davids, Oxford
University Press, London, 1921.) The goal to be sought is
not momentary elation, but an enduring, universal, omni-
present enjoyment: '. . . unshakeable freedom of mind, this

is the goal. . . .' (*The Middle Length Sayings*, Vol. I, p. 253.) When achieved, then 'to whatever place you go, you shall go in comfort; wherever you stand, you shall stand in comfort; wherever you sit, you shall sit in comfort; and wherever you make your bed, you shall lie down in comfort.' (*The Book of the Gradual Sayings*, Vol. IV, p. 200. See *ibid.*, Vol. V, p. 83.)

The problem, which presents itself in life and in the Pali record in multifarious ways, may be stated thus: 'For the most part, monks, beings wish like this: "O may pleasant, enjoyable, agreeable things grow much." Monks, unpleasant, unenjoyable, disagreeable things grow much in those beings of such wishes. . . . Why is this? or What do you take to be the cause?' (*The Middle Length Sayings*, Vol. I, p. 372.) Gotama's answer is commonly summarized as the 'Four Truths' or the 'Four Certainties'.

These are not four different principles, but a single principle, the factors or strands of which may be analysed and numbered in as many ways as suits one's fancy. It seems better to believe that Gotama did not, like a numerologist, attach special significance to numbers, but that the prominence they play in the formulas grew naturally out of the interests of memorizers needing convenient fingerable numbers to assist them in mental bookkeeping. As internal evidence, one may appeal to the spirit of the principle itself as it inspires any life lived in accordance with it. Concern for freedom from anxiety involves a deep and earnest yearning pervading one's whole being in such a way that mnemonic numbering seems highly artificial by contrast. Following this principle dialectically, however, one would neither be greatly attached to nor greatly abhor enumerations. Yet enumeration of, elaboration of, devoted attention to, each of the four, and especially the eight steps of the fourth, subtly but progressively distract the quester from focusing upon the principle itself. Details, when multiplied, obscure the simplicity and intuitive clarity of the central doctrine. Even though, in orthodox versions, the steps are described as leading progressively toward the goal of concentration in *nirvana*, *nirvana* is conceived as objectless, and subjectless, cessation of all activity, and the description is suffused with a spirit of seeking to live for the sake of concentration rather than of seeking concentration for the sake of life. A step-wise procedure, especially one which meanders throughout the gamut of personal and social duties, positive and negative (including belief, resolve, speech, conduct, livelihood, endeavour, mindfulness, and concentration), and which, even if it did get to the goal at last, would do so only indirectly (even after several rebirths and a life devoted to monkish living), is not the sort of thing which Gotama would recommend. He always led his hearers back, in a most direct fashion, to the principle itself. More devious discussions, when they occurred, were for the purpose of getting the hearer's confidence that his problem was being grasped sympathetically and adequately and for clarifying the contexts to show that, even in the specific context of the hearer's own problem, there was a place from which to deduce the relevance, soundness, and sufficiency of his principle.

Furthermore, the middle way, named explicitly in many of the formulas, is lost in the process. Despite repetition of *sam*—equanimity (*see* below, Ch. 7)—originally intended as re-emphasizing that everything, no matter how many different kinds of things, should be interpreted middle-wayedly (and kept later as a mnemonic introduction to each of the eight steps in all standard formulas), the middle way was gradually smothered by a tendency toward one extreme. The ideal of temperance, moderation, calmness, freedom

from anxiety, involving avoidance of attachment to either
desire or stopping of desire, gave way to the ideal of
abstinence, abstemiousness, extinction of all desire, and
extinction even of the desirer and of his life. This negativistic, nihilistic spirit, expressed aptly in English word-play,
avoid all but the void, was explicitly repudiated by Gotama:
'There are recluses and brahmans who misrepresent me untruly, vainly, falsely, not in accordance with fact, saying:
"The recluse Gotama is a nihilist, he lays down the cutting
off, the destruction, the disappearance of existent entity."
But as this, monks, is just what I am not, as this is just what
I do not say, therefore these worthy recluses and brahmans
misrepresent me untruly. . . .' (*The Middle Length Sayings*,
Vol. I, p. 180.)

Nevertheless, this negativistic spirit took over and per-
vaded Buddhist thought if not in his own time, at least at
times centuries later. Unsympathetic critics pounce with
glee upon such negativism as demonstrating Buddhism's
inferiority to more positive, life-affirming philosophies and
religions. But, not only in the thought of Gotama, but in
most branches of Buddhist philosophy, there are saving
features which must be given their due. And, in practical
religion, not only does life itself so necessarily reject self-
annihilation that nihilism cannot be practised without
modification, but also Buddhism, judging by the multitudes
of compromises it has made in the various cultures it has
penetrated, even dominated, has proved itself to be one of
the world's most adaptable religions. Granted that a negative element is present, it does not follow that nihilism is
essential to Buddhism. Granted that stopping of desire and
stopping of the desire to stop desire tend to result in an
indifference to life which is difficult to distinguish from
negation of life, one can appreciate Buddhism adequately

only if he is willing to see the distinction as subtle rather than vague and remember that both Gotama and most practising Buddhists rebel against negativity for the sake of negativity (just as Jews and Christians explain their negative 'Thou shalt not' commandments as leading intentionally to a positive goal). This subtlety, which is missed by simpler Buddhists, is here interpreted as not mere stopping of desire, but as stopping of desire for more than one will attain. This latter clause, expressing something so obvious as to seem not to need explicit statement, when forgotten, turns an affirmation into a negation. Gotama's principle affirms acceptance of what is, indeed, all of what is (in all tenses of 'to be'), by denying that one can have other than, i.e., a degree of negation of, what is. But one can retain awareness of this subtlety only if he refuses to let himself be led away from it down the steps of an eight-step path.

Although it is true that within Buddhist cultures the steps may be used to guide beginners and the immature in step-wise growth, and different teachers have exercised great ingenuity in incorporating all needed moral principles and codes into their interpretation of it, any mistaking of such an eight-step path for the middle way (*see below*, Ch. 7, for another interpretation) is to lead one away from the source and mainstay of Buddhism. That some teachers use the eight-step path to lead their pupils back to the middle way is certainly to their credit. But the spirit of step-wise progressing, going from one end of a series to the other, aiming at perfecting or terminating the series, has extremism inherent in it. Perfectionism entails extremism, for one cannot achieve perfection without going all the way to the end, the extreme.

Does Buddhism escape the evils of perfectionism? Some forms of Buddhism do not. Succumbing to the powerful pull of directionism inherent in stepping progressively, they conceive the eighth and last step, *samadhi*, sometimes merely as cessation, but oftener as involving several (usually four) additional steps or *jhanas* before reaching the ultimate goal of perfect steplessness. Other forms of Buddhism do escape by transcending the end, not by going beyond the end of the series into nowhere (nihilism), but by transcending the series as serial. These forms then naturally involve themselves in an 'all-ism' rather than a nihilism. Some of them then succumb to an extreme or perfectionistic all-ism. (E.g., Madhyamika.) But others, following a middle course between all-ism and nihilism, find themselves involved, dialectically, in another all (inclusive of both all-ism and nihilism) which in turn can avoid perfectionism only by further dialectical transcendence, without succumbing, as Hegel did, to a dialectical Absolute terminating dialectic. How far this escape can be read into the record as being clearly or vaguely in Gotama's mind remains a matter of guessing. But at least his principle has inherent in it the power to escape the death which lies in waiting, not so much at the end of an eight-step path as at the beginning, since it is the directionism inherent in the first step that is death to that attitude which accepts what is (in all senses of 'to be') as itself the goal.

This power to escape is the power of the principle of the middle way to transcend without going beyond (destroying or leaving behind) itself. Three aspects of such transcendence may be noted: (*a*) The whole series may be transcended, not by stepping out beyond the last step, but by transcending the series as serial. One experiences the path in a different dimension when he both desires and desires to stop desiring no more nor less than he will achieve, not by desiring to take each step in turn until he takes the last step into desirelessness, but by neither desiring nor desiring to stop desiring to progress more than he will progress up the eight-step path. That is, only by becoming indifferent to the step-wise character of the path can one achieve its goal, its transcendental goal (which is, at the same time, its intrinsic goal). (*b*) Each of the eight steps may itself be middle-wayed, or transcended dialectically on its own account. Introduced by *sam*, meaning 'middle-wayed', each may be interpreted, not as an ordinary step, but as another transcendental step, mentioned separately not to give significance to it as separate, but to illustrate or demonstrate the all-pervasiveness of the principle. That this is true is so incomprehensible to beginners, and so unbelievable to those whose faith in the formulas has remained unshaken by penetrative reflection, that much doubt must remain on the part of many readers. This aspect of the eight-fold path is of such significance that it will receive more detailed treatment later. (*See* Ch. 7.) (*c*) Stepness can be transcended from the very beginning or, even, before the beginning, by anyone who grasps the principle intuitively and acquiesces in it immediately. This grasping and acquiescing is the ideal, but few achieve it. Unfortunately for this ideal, life is directional. All men desire more than they will get, hence all are frustrated, and all, then, must take some steps away from such desiring. But that there should be precisely eight steps is not a consequence of the principle itself. Some will require more, some less; but the fewer the better. If some are so inept as to require several rounds of rebirth, what can be done about it? Not even the teacher can wish that his pupils would speed up their process more than they will without he himself succumbing to desiring more than he will get.

The Buddhist monk is, and usually knows that he is,

in a most precarious position. Not only does donning the yellow robe require considerable commitment to devotion to the way, but his degree of commitment may itself be his worst enemy. For any degree of avidity for success beyond what will be achieved is the very evil which he must seek to uproot. Not only must he carefully prejudge whether or not the theory is too subtle for his comprehension but also whether or not he himself is competent and ready for this kind of achievement. If he has been pressured into acceptance by proud parents desiring a saint for a son, his chances of success may have been greatly diminished. He must commit himself to accepting the possibility that he will make little progress and that he will be satisfied with however little he makes. He commits himself also to accepting the fact that he will be misunderstood, especially by those worldly perfectionists (not themselves perfect, or capable of perfection, but expecting exemplary behaviour from others) who are quick to cry 'hypocrite' at those not measuring up to their own unpractised and impracticable ideals. He may even have to commit himself to being as hypocritical as he will have to be. He may, for example, have to say, for the benefit of those who require him to speak, that he has committed himself more than he has, or less than he has, in order that he may have the opportunity to continue to commit himself as much as he has.

Putting off the yellow robe, which may be done at any time, is not to be considered a great catastrophe. Whatever regrets an ex-monk may have should be directed not so much to having tried and failed, but to having desired to try before he was ready. If he succeeds in stopping such regretting, he may, by that act, achieve more success in accordance with the principle than he did during his whole career as a monk. External observers, shocked by the very ordinary behaviour of some monks, fail to recognize that conformity to prescribed behaviour patterns is an irrelevancy which must be acceded to only because, in the particular cultural system in which he actually lives, life according to these rules is what he is going to get anyway and he would merely be frustrating himself unnecessarily by not accepting them. Critics who wonder whether a monk then might not be free to commit all sorts of crimes, so long as he is willing to accept the fact and consequences of his being a criminal, themselves must belong to that class of little cheaters who have not yet learned that one cannot trifle with truth. Crimes he may commit, but only those which he honestly thinks are not crimes. (Cf. *The Book of the Discipline*, Part IV, pp. 483–6. Tr. I. B. Horner, Luzac and Co., Ltd., London, 1951.) Monk and critic alike, who are not willing to be completely honest, i.e., complete in the dialectical sense of being honestly willing to be also as dishonest as they are, can expect little but disappointment from their half-hearted pursuit of the middle way.

Further paradoxical evidence regarding the uncertain character of the eight-fold path is to be found in its startling omission from the 'Book of the Eights', an exhaustive collection of items listed together in groups of eight which were remembered at the time of final compilation. (*See The Book of the Gradual Sayings*, Vol. IV.) A lone mention of the bare list as eight 'states' 'for the complete understanding of passion' in an apparently appended last chapter suggests that, even at the time of appending, the eight were not conceived as steps in a significant eight-fold path. (Cf. *ibid.*, p. 229.) Furthermore, the list, with two steps added, namely 'right knowledge' and 'right release', not only appears in the 'Book of the Tens', probably a somewhat later compilation, but is repeated at least once in each of sixty-two consecutively recorded sections or suttas. (Cf. *The Book of the Gradual Sayings*, Vol. V, Chs. XI–XVI, Sections 103–66, pp. 149–70.) Here is a sample of this list of ten: 'Monks, for a man, a person, who has wrong view, wrong thinking, speech, action, living, effort, mindfulness, concentration, wrong knowledge and wrong release, whatsoever bodily action is carried to completion and fulfilment according to that view, whatsoever activities of the mind (directed thereto) there may be—all those states conduce to what is unpleasant, not delightful, not charming, not profitable, to what is painful.' (*Ibid.*, p. 150. *See also The Book of the Kindred Sayings*, Vol. V, p. 18.)

In many other collections where the eight-fold path is mentioned, it is treated with relative insignificance, as, for example, in the Maha-sukuludayi sutta (Cf. *Further Dialogues of the Buddha*, Vol. II, pp. 6–12), where it is listed as merely one of nineteen sets of ways (or as eight out of more than seventy-five items) useful in achieving the goal. In one sutta giving it a central place, it is treated as subordinate to 'three classes', i.e., moral habit, concentration and intuitive wisdom: 'The three classes are not arranged in accordance with the ariyan eight-fold way, but the ariyan eight-fold way is arranged in accordance with the three classes. Whatever is perfect speech, whatever is perfect action, whatever is perfect way of living—these are arranged in the class of Moral Habit. And whatever is perfect behaviour and whatever is perfect mindfulness and whatever is perfect concentration—these things are arranged in the class of Concentration. And whatever is perfect view and whatever is perfect thought—these things are arranged in the class of Intuitive Wisdom.' (*The Middle Length Sayings*, Vol. I, p. 363.) Not a single example is to be found where the eight-step path is treated in a spirit exuding vitality and common sense. Granted that

such treatments are rare in the mass of the Pitakas, nevertheless if the eight-step path did in fact originate with Gotama,
one might hope to find somewhere a remembered example
of a living, breathing context in which it was expounded.
And in none is the spirit of the middle way expressed (even
mention of it is omitted from many expositions!); in those
suttas where elaboration of the meaning of the formula is
attempted, there is a tendency in the direction of Theravada
doctrine, characterized both by a spirit of enumeration and
of extreme abstinence (as in the Sacca-Vibhanga sutta;
Further Dialogues of the Buddha, Vol. II, pp. 296–9). Mrs.
Rhys Davids suggests that the formulas of the four truths
and the eight-fold path were drafted too late for inclusion
in the 'Book of the Fours' and 'Book of the Eights'. (*See*
C. A. F. Rhys Davids, *The Book of the Gradual Sayings*,
Vol. IV, pp. x, xii; and *Gotama, the Man*, pp. 99, 220.
Luzac and Co., Ltd., London, 1928.) Although the thesis of
this book does not require that the doctrine of an eight-step
path was unknown to Gotama, it does imply that the view
that there are exactly eight steps, or even any number of
steps, is not essential to his philosophy. Of course, since life
is in fact directional, one who is willing to accept things as
they are in fact is also willing to accept steps wherever they
are needed. But the core of Gotama's doctrine is not that
there are eight steps to *nirvana*, nor, even, four distinguish-
able truths, but that there is one ultimate principle regarding
happiness: to stop frustration, stop desiring what will not
be attained.

4

DESIRE AND FRUSTRATION

Two types of theories concerning the way to end frustration are: (1) To stop frustration, stop desire. (2) To stop frustration, stop desiring what will not be attained. The first type takes two forms: (*a*) To stop desire, remove the objects stimulating desire. (*b*) To stop desire, stop desiring. Each of these three solutions will be considered in turn.

To end frustration, stop desire; and to stop desire, remove the objects stimulating desire. The goal is the source of the aim; remove the goal and you remove the aim. This is, indeed, a simple solution, and, no matter how childish it may seem from certain standpoints, it is one that not only is commonly, persistently and easily practised, but one which will retain a fundamental place in any final solution.

Part of the appeal of this theory is not only its immediate obviousness as a theory but its widespread effectiveness in practice. Objects of which one is unaware can hardly arouse his interest. Remove from one's environment, or remove one from the environment of, desirable objects, and the desire itself tends to disappear—as summed up in the saying, 'Out of sight, out of mind.' The enormous expenditures for advertising are justified by, and serve as justification for, this principle. Parental warding of children and political warding of citizens appear to depend for success upon using this principle wisely. Primitive peoples seem happier with little than millionaires who commit suicide despite their much.

The Pali record is replete with advice regarding withdrawal of objects from the senses (seek solitude in forest or cave) as well as of the senses from objects. Statement of the principle may be illustrated thus: 'It is out of the question and impossible to get a fire to blaze up without fuel, except by a magician's art. The fire that is kindled with fuel symbolizes the satisfaction which arises from pleasures of sense; while the fire without fuel symbolizes the satisfaction which arises when pleasures of sense and wrong dispositions are not.' (*Further Dialogues of the Buddha*, Vol. II, p. 117.) No little part of both the theory's obviousness and effectiveness is the way it accounts for differences in degree of desire: remove the most intensely desired objects and one's interest will then be occupied with less intensely desired objects. Justification of homelessness, mendicancy, and celibacy for monks rests partly on this principle. 'Monks, I see no other single form so enticing, so desirable, so intoxicating, so distracting, such a hindrance to the winning of unsurpassed peace from effort—that is to say, monks, as a woman's form.' (*The Book of the Gradual Sayings*, Vol. III, p. 56.)

However, this theory, despite its apparent obviousness and effectiveness in some areas, is not a complete solution. It overlooks other equally fundamental and obvious facts. Some objects cannot be removed, such as the stars, the weather, and a neighbour's wife. Some desires persist even in the absence of their objects, and cause us to go in search of the objects. Memory, habit, instinct remain even when objects are absent. Furthermore, desires often originate from internal causes: hunger, thirst, and sex desires arise without external stimulus. And one's dream desires and satisfactions may surpass those of waking life. It is not true, universally, that to remove the object is to remove the desire. Since only some desires can be thus removed, i.e., those which do actually depend on an object for their origin, one must seek elsewhere for a more adequate solution.

The second solution, even more profusely suggested in the Pali records, is like the first in seeking to end frustration by stopping desire. But its method is this: to stop desire, stop desiring. Stated thus tautologically, the theory appears even more simple and obvious, logically, than the first one which, by comparison, is indirect, requiring all sorts of other desires and efforts to remove the objects. This theory assumes that one has free spontaneous control over his own desires; all that is needed is sufficient exercise of will, and the task is accomplished. A self which desires voluntarily can voluntarily stop desiring. 'It is just like a man who, being violently in love with a woman, sees her standing about and chatting and laughing with another man. Would the sight pain him and make him miserable?' 'Yes sir: because he is so violently in love with her that he would be very much pained at the sight.' 'Suppose now this man were to reflect that, being violently in love with the woman, he had been much distressed by seeing her with another man, and that consequently he would do well to rid himself of his love for her. Suppose he does so and later on sees her laughing and talking with another. Would the sight still pain him and make him miserable?' 'No sir: because he has lost all his old passion for her and therefore does not mind.' (*Further Dialogues of the Buddha*, Vol. II, p. 128.)

If, as is so often the case, one has difficulty in succeeding all at once, he will have to approach his goal bit by bit. When he lacks sufficient control over his desires to eliminate them immediately and completely, then he must stalk his prey with stealth and steadiness. Furthermore, the task, in practice, is not just control over desire, generally, but over desires, all of them, and each in turn. Hence, Buddhist monks, after their social and physiological requirements have been taken care of, either by fulfilling them fully willingly or by abandoning them acceptably, begin their gradual practices by laboriously mastering each of the senses in turn, so the many desires stimulatable through each may be brought under voluntary control. When this task has been achieved, then the desires stimulated by memory, imagination and reflective thought must be conquered likewise. Only then, after all the specific types of desire have been so mastered, is one ready to conquer desire itself—desire in general as against specific desires. Since here also there are degrees or stages, one must still proceed a step at a time, through the *jhanas* interpreted as stages approaching complete cessation of desire.

Turning to difficulties with this second solution, so simple in theory and seemingly practicable—even if requiring years of monkly practice—we should examine other facts, ignored or minimized by both foregoing theories, which, when considered, will be seen to be also fundamental and ineradicable in their own way. These facts are of two sorts or give support to two statements: It is impossible to stop desiring. Nobody really wants to stop desiring. Relative to the first, facts will be classified as 'experiential', 'inferential', and 'dialectical'.

1. Evidence for the contention that it is impossible to stop desiring may be found first by consulting experience. Surely one never catches himself not desiring, except in rare moments of seemingly complete satisfaction, whether of ecstasy or repose. And such moments, no matter how complete and timeless they may appear from within the moment, endure for but a moment and then disappear like a whitecap

in a sea of desires. Even if one could prolong such a moment enough to give internal attention to it as such, he would find inherent in his anticipation of prolongation a forward look, a desire for, or a willingness to have, a future, which look-desire-willingness is not wholly contented with, not completely convinced about the all-sufficiency of, the timeless present. Experience testifies that one is never wholly without desire for long—for long enough to know about it. Both the inner and outer (eternal and temporal, complete and incomplete, satisfactory and unsatisfactory, calm and anxious) appearances constitute ultimate parts of the whole truth about a moment of experience. Neither alone (the inner, as with Advaitins, Jains, Samkhyans, Yogins, and many Buddhists; or the outer, as with Romanticists, especially Existentialists, and with Instrumentalists) is ultimate. If this be so, then those who idealize the inner alone as ultimate, in reality or in value, are as mistaken as those who eulogize the outer alone.

The efforts of bhikkhus, those most thoroughly devoted to this philosophy, testify to its practical difficulties. Novices are admitted at very early ages, because sometimes years of study and practice are required before one can begin to comprehend the subtleties of the steps, theoretical and practical, into ultimate desirelessness. The fortnightly *Patimokkha*, or public recitation and confession regarding the two hundred and twenty-seven rules and infractions thereof, is considered a necessary aid for most monks. Backsliding continues to be a constant danger during all but the last stages. Monks still have desires; and some desires, such as those for food, air, elimination, and rest, persist throughout life. To live is to desire. 'Hope springs eternal. . . .' The experiences of the reader himself, and the testimony of monks, yield evidence for the contention that it is impossible to stop desiring. Only the higher stages of *jhana*, which are both rare and admittedly beyond the range of ordinary experience (and which may have other better explanations than that they lead to complete cessation), remain as contrary evidence.

2. Facts here classified as 'inferential' refer to two types of inference: the first, physiological, pertaining to emotions, the second, ontological, pertaining to being and its survival tendency.

If, as physiologists tell us, there is an intimate relation between desire and emotion (e.g., as in the James-Lange theory of emotions: we are afraid because we cry, rather than cry because we are afraid), the theory that there can be complete cessation of desire must reckon with, refute or revise, physiological theory before its case can be considered established. Although one may, for his private purposes, ignore such theory, he can expect little public hearing until he has come forth with more convincing contrary evidence in this area. If to live is to have emotions and to have emotions is to have desires, then one can hardly have complete cessation of desire and yet live.

Being, some ontologists believe, involves an inherent tendency to continue. Such tendency is directional, directed from the present to the future, or from present being to future being. Such directionality may be interpreted as purposive, where purpose consists in one thing (or a thing at one time) finding its goal in something else (or in the same thing at another time). If anything had its whole being only in itself at a moment, it would be purposeless, nondirectional, non-temporal, and, at least according to some ontologists, non-being. Belief in the basicness of such a tendency is supported not only by the reasoning of ontologists, but by evidence from biology ('instinct for survival',

'survival is nature's first law'), physics ('law of inertia', 'principle of the conservation of energy'), theology (ideals concerning 'eternality of God' and 'immortality of the soul'). Even various Buddhistic doctrines, such as *bhavanga* (Theravadin concept of a ceaseless flow of subconscious being) and *bodhi* (Mahayanic concept of Buddha as an eternal cosmic principle of enlightened being), appear to presuppose that this tendency to continue is a characteristic of ultimate being. Now whenever such a tendency becomes conscious, it is experienced as purpose or desire—using these terms in their broadest sense. If there can be no continuing consciousness, or consciousness of continuing, without such desire, why idealize continuing consciousness completely void of desire, when all that is wanted, really, is avoidance of frustration? Carried to its logical conclusions, the ideal of complete cessation of desire ends either in pessimism, a conclusion drawn by Schopenhauer and some Hindus, or in nihilism, the seeds of which are present in the ingeniously rationalized no-soul and no-substance (*anatta* and *anicca*) doctrines presupposing that the self, its desires, and the objects desired, have no reality as such in the first place. Since neither Gotama himself nor Buddhists generally have drawn these nihilistic and pessimistic conclusions, surely they cannot really accept, no matter how much at times they may seem to be accepting, complete cessation of desire as their ultimate goal.

3. Facts classified here as 'dialectical' refer to the impossibility of desiring to stop desiring without thereby desiring. Also, dialectically, if to have succeeded in stopping desire is to have satisfied the desire to stop desiring, then, in the enjoyment of this satisfaction as satisfaction of desire, is not the desire still present at least implicitly? (*See* Ch. 8 for further treatment of dialectic.)

Finally, let us consider the fact that no one really wants to stop desiring, even if he could. For, apart from desire, in the most general sense of the term, there are no values. *Nirvana* is the ultimate goal because it is the ultimate value. And it is the ultimate value because it is the ultimate in desirability. It ought to be desired and, as the highest good, it ought to be desired above all other goods. Not cessation of desire, but desiring the most desirable—this is the goal of man, and of Gotama, and of Buddhism. Such cessation as is advocated is a means to an end, not the end itself. It is because this goal is believed so desirable that desires for all lesser goals should cease. Bhikkus, even though they may succeed in keeping themselves at a low level of excitement, do, nevertheless, enjoy life, both by satisfying many ordinary desires and by feeling some satisfaction that they are making progress toward their ultimate goal. Most of them are sustained by a faith or confidence that the ultimate in desirability is obtainable for them, or has already been attained by them. One can only guess as to what part is played in supporting this confidence by a feeling of pride (satisfying the desire for esteem), inspired by praise from superiors, from the public, expressed or inferred, or from their own estimation of progress made as measured by the standards set by their Order for achieving progress, and what part is played by a subconscious conviction that success in cessation of desire is really success in satisfaction of desire. If *nirvana* were undesirable, striving for it would be futile and senseless. The fact that bhikkus feel that the struggle not only makes sense, but is, for them, most worth while, implies not that they want to stop desiring but that they desire what is most desirable.

The third solution, although not always so clearly expressed in the Pali scriptures, nevertheless appears a more satisfactory interpretation both of the nature of desire and frustration and of certain significant passages in the scriptures than either of the first two theories. This solution aims not at removing frustration by removing desire but by desiring only those objects which will bring satisfaction. Once stated, this solution also, as a theory, appears obvious both logically and psychologically: If you desire those desires which will be satisfied, you will be satisfied; if you desire those desires which will be frustrated, you will be frustrated. Therefore, desire those desires which will be satisfied; cease desiring those which will be frustrated. 'It is just like a man hunting about for milk, in his need and quest for milk, who should milk a young cow from her horn, yet for all his pains he cannot draw milk therefrom. . . . And why not? Because it is not the source from which milk can come.' (*Further Dialogues of the Buddha*, Vol II, p. 237.)

However, this leaves unresolved the problem of which desires to have, and how to find out which desires can be satisfied and which not. Desires do not come already labelled: 'to be satisfied' or 'to be frustrated'. Furthermore, sometimes satisfactions and frustrations come tied together, as when faced with a necessary choice between two or more equally desirable alternatives, only one of which can be enjoyed. Also, satisfaction is a matter of degree; one may expect more or less satisfaction than he gets, and enjoy his surprise at the outcome. In face of uncertainty, the desire to predict and to have confidence in one's predictions naturally arises, and the thrills of making successful predictions, and of taking risks, may themselves constitute satisfactions regardless of the outcome. Life is a gamble, and some seem to get much extra enjoyment from being able to take greater risks than their fellows. Desires which are long in the fulfilling may be accompanied by much anticipation, and the pleasures of anticipatory imaginative fulfilment may be greater, more rewarding, than those of actual achievement. The joy of progress toward a goal is a harvest reaped even though the goal itself is never reached. 'To travel hopefully is better than to arrive.' (Robert Louis Stevenson in *El Dorado*.) Also, some satisfactions seem greater if accompanied either by frustration or fear of frustration (bad, by contrast, makes some good better). Finally, there appear to be masochists who seem to desire and enjoy suffering. So, although this theory is logically and psychologically simple, it also may be seen to encounter a whole forest of psychological obstacles.

One may reply, in defence of this theory, that people do in fact learn from experience which kinds of desires cannot be realized, which have greater probability of satisfaction, and which can be satisfied to a greater degree. If this is not true for all areas of life, at least it is for some; so a person, instead of trying to stop desiring altogether, will seek to herd his desires into greener pastures. In fact, growing up, maturing, psychologically and morally, consists in just this: accumulating a greater wealth of satisfiable desires. The purpose of psychiatry and morality is to help people to act in such a way as to get the most satisfaction from the least effort (frustration). (Theories of morality which violate this principle are themselves immoral.) It is true that some persons profit by experience more easily than others, but all, even most animals, can learn something from experience. Some cultures, with their systems of government, education, morality, religion, and science, promote such learning more than do others. Search for such better cultures should replace search for a way to stop desiring. One can desire and take extra satisfaction in having achieved a new or higher level of morality, of satisfaction without frustration, of automatic rather than conscience-stricken inhibition, of desire for what he will get. One may interpret the purpose of religious life, of bhikkus and laymen alike, as devoted to the desire to progress in, and enjoyment of satisfaction in making progress in, increasing limitation of desires to those most likley to be satisfied. Surely this is a much healthier interpretation of the record attributed to Gotama. *Nirvana* consists in optimum satisfaction, not in absence of both frustration and satisfaction.

But how, then, shall we interpret such statements as 'Destruction of craving is *Nibbana*'? (*The Book of the Kindred Sayings*, Vol. III, p. 157. Tr. F. L. Woodward, Luzac and Co., Ltd., London, 1925, 1954.) The spirit of the complete-cessation ideal saturates the Pali scriptures, and yet so many of the examples, and attempts at explanation, given therein refer not to desire but to desirousness, not to wanting, but to craving, not to getting, but to being greedy, not to accepting, but to clinging. Gotama's doctrine centres not upon destruction of desire, but upon destruction of craving. It pertains to 'anguish and the stopping of anguish' (*The Middle Length Sayings*, Vol. I, p. 180), to frustration, not to desire and the stopping of desire. 'Just as when boys and girls play with little sand-castles. So long as they are not rid of lust, nor rid of desire, nor rid of affection, thirst, feverish longing and craving for those little sand-castles, just so long do they delight in them, are amused by them, set store by them, are jealous of them. But as soon as . . . rid . . . of craving for those little sand-castles, straightway with hand and foot they scatter them, break them up, knock them down, cease to play with them.' (*The Book of the Kindred Sayings*, Vol. III, pp. 156–7.) Cravings can be eradicated as completely as sand-castles. Surely it is easier to eradicate cravings, excessive desires, than to eliminate all desire? Or is it?

5

CRAVING

THUS far we have postponed facing directly the problem of distinguishing precisely between desiring and craving. That there is a distinction to be made is clear. But can distinction be made clearly? Is the difference one of kind or of degree?

The view that the distinction is one of kind has its advocates. Some Buddhists differentiate sharply between *tanha* and *chanda*. *Tanha* represents anxiety in all its forms: craving, greed, thirst, impetuosity, obstinacy, avidity, revulsion, hankering, fear, conceit, envy, vexation, anger. (Cf. *The Middle Length Sayings*, Vol. I, pp. 15–16.) *Chanda* usually refers to desire without anxiety, to desires regarding which no question, no uncertainty, no fear, is aroused concerning their satisfaction, as when, on a quiet stroll, one puts one leg forward at a time because he wants to. But *chanda* is especially difficult to define because, like the English word 'desire', it also embodies enough breadth and ambiguity of meaning to include anxieties also. For example: '. . . five kinds of *chanda*: desire to seek, to gain, to enjoy, to hoard, to spend, and includes all in the present connection with the words: "here it is used in a sense tantamount to craving (*tanha*)." ' (T. W. and C. A. F. Rhys Davids in *Dialogues of the Buddha*, Part II, p. 311, footnote. Oxford University Press, London, 1910. Luzac and Co., Ltd., London, 1919, 1951.) The distinction between *chanda* and *tanha* may best be thought of as akin to the difference between desire and desirousness or between will and wilfulness, which involves at once both a difference in kind and a difference in degree. Difference in kind may appear more obvious when it is recalled that will, for example, ambiguously connotes both willingness and wilfulness, both passive, permissive, submissive will and active, assertive, aggressive will. Permitting and insisting, or consenting and demanding, though opposites, both express will or desire.

However, more careful attention to the meanings of these terms reduces their sharpness as different in kind. The view that their difference is one of kind appeals to those who would like to have a simple and easy solution to the predicament under consideration. If craving (*tanha*) leads to frustration whereas desire (*chanda*) does not, then all that is needed is to distinguish between them in each case and we will have our 'to be satisfied' and 'to be frustrated' labels before us. 'It comes to this then that the one goes with the other; with violence of effort you suffer pain and anguish, whereas without that violence you do not.' (*Further Dialogues of the Buddha*, Vol. II, p. 126.)

Nevertheless, actual practice confronts us oftener with difference in degree. Craving is simply excessive desire. When is desire in excess? The same desire, such as becoming hungry before mealtime, at first manifests itself as *chanda* ('Well, it must be about time to eat'), and then changes gradually, as one waits longer and longer and gets hungrier and hungrier, into *tanha* ('What's keeping the waiter? I can't stand it any longer!). The most simple and innocent desires have a way of turning suddenly into demands, as when food, even monotonously conveyed to the mouth, suddenly slips from the fork, or as when indifference to a dog explodes into fear of his death before an onrushing vehicle. Desire to keep a trinket, although diminished almost to indifference, flares up violently if it is stolen from us. Even those utterly bored with life get excited when suddenly faced with death. Furthermore, some desires, through being satisfied, become established as an urge for repetition, and some, being repeatedly satisfied, turn into gnawing anxieties when unfulfilled. Hence, the distinction between desire and craving is primarily one of degree, and is a difference which is seldom clear. Great differences such as those between a whim and a tantrum merely represent extremes in a scale of degrees, for the same wish may express itself first as whim and then as tantrum. One need only observe children at play, if he cannot mirror his own development, in order to be convinced of this generalization.

Concluding that the distinction between desire and craving is one of degree does not settle the problem of how to get rid of craving. It merely relocates the problem in such a way that any adequate solution must be one which can deal with such differences, even slight differences, in degree. This conclusion involves recognition that the problem, in practice, is perpetually difficult and that constant alertness to it is needed. Its recurrence is so persistent and so provoking that the desire to end desire is not wholly unjustified. One must forgive speakers, interpreters, memorizers, and translators if the precise degree of difference intended is not always clearly conveyed. From the standpoint of formulating a theory about it, the problem is slippery to handle and anyone insisting on grasping it with tong-like firmness is doomed to disappointment. Yet this is life's most important problem and cannot be evaded except by defeatists, and defeatism itself is not so much an evasion as a solution. Surprisingly enough, the very willingness to face the problem, no matter how difficult it will turn out to be, itself provides the clue to its solution. In accepting the problem for what it is, one already is expressing willingness to accept things as they are. Gotama's principle, stop desiring what will not be obtained, is an intellectualized formulation of the willingness to face life as it is.

Regardless of whether the difference between desire and craving is one of degree or kind (the record appears never to be wholly clear about the matter), interpreting Gotama's doctrine as aiming at cessation of craving seems much saner and healthier than extinction of all desire or, worse, extinction of self, or, even, of all existence. Failure of the record, or of its readers, to discern that craving, not desire, is diagnosed as the cause of suffering, has opened the way for differences of opinion and schools of thought among orthodox Buddhists. All of them, without exception, however, agree that craving ends in suffering and that Gotama dealt with craving: 'Gotama: pray how far is *Dhamma* seen in this life? How far is it a thing not involving time . . .?' 'Brahmin, one who is ablaze with lust, overwhelmed with lust, infatuated thereby, plans to his own hindrance, to that of others, to the hindrance of both self and others, and experiences mental suffering and dejection. If lust be abandoned, he no longer plans thus, no longer suffers thus. So far, brahmin, *Dhamma* is seen in this life.' (*The Book of the Gradual Sayings*, Vol. I, p. 140. Tr. F. L. Woodward, Luzac and Co., Ltd., London, 1932, 1951.) The following, although apparently a later poetical overstatement, expresses the ideal in extreme: 'The bliss of lusts and heaven-world equal not one sixteenth of the bliss of craving's ending.' (*The Minor Anthologies of the Pali Canon*, Vol. II, p. 14.)

Gotama's hearers, although immediately impressed and amazed by his discourses,[3] also reflecting upon and discussing with one another what he had said, came to him again and again inquiring about applications of his principle to different practical problems. He obliged each in turn by examining his specific problem, but always trying to make clear that the principle itself, and not the example merely, was important.

The remainder of the present chapter is devoted to some illustrations of application of the principle to practical problems in various areas of life: possessions, pride, loved ones, sensuous pleasures, and mental values.

Craving for possessions takes many forms: making, getting, keeping, consuming. There is no harm in seeking things, so long as they are things one can have without such craving. Business men, for example, desire profits. Discussing the conditions leading to a 'clansman's advantage and happiness here on earth', Gotama reputedly named 'the even life. Herein a clansman, while experiencing both gain and loss in wealth, continues his business serenely not unduly elated or depressed. Thinks he: "Thus my income, after deducting the loss, will stand (at so much) and my outgoings will not exceed my income." Just as one who carries scales, or his apprentice, knows, on holding up the balance, that either by so much it has dipped down or by so much it has tilted up; even so, a clansman experiencing both gain and loss continues his business serenely, neither unduly

---

[3] E.g., '. . . clever nobles, subtle, practised in disputing with others, skilled in hair-splitting . . . construct a question, thinking: Having approached the recluse Gotama, we will ask him this question of ours. If . . . he answers thus, we will refute him thus; and if . . . he answers thus, we will refute him thus. . . . The recluse Gotama gladdened, roused, incited, delighted them with his talk on *dhamma*. These . . . did not ask the recluse Gotama the question at all—whence could they refute him? On the contrary they became disciples of the recluse Gotama.' (*The Middle Length Sayings*, Vol. I, p. 221.)

elated nor unduly depressed. . . .' (*The Book of the Gradual Sayings*, Vol IV, pp. 187, 188–9.)

Pride, which 'goeth before the fall', is avoided by the happy man. 'I have naught to do with homage, Nagita, nor has homage aught to do with me. Whosoever cannot obtain at will, easily and without difficulty, this happiness of seclusion, this happiness of calm, this happiness of awakening, which I can obtain at will, easily and without difficulty; let him enjoy that midden of happiness, that dung-like happiness, that happiness gotten of gains, favours and flattery.' (*The Book of the Gradual Sayings*, Vol. IV, pp. 224–5.) To one who has 'found the highest goal . . . there comes no thought: "There is one better than", nor "There is one equal", nor "There is one worse"'. (*Ibid.*, Vol. III, p. 255. Tr. E. M. Hare, Luzac and Co., Ltd., London, 1934, 1952.) 'Be ye not measurers of persons, take not the measure of persons. A person is ruined by taking the measure of other persons.' (*The Book of the Gradual Sayings*, Vol. V, p. 97.)

Attachment to loved ones, in some ways the richest and most rewarding aspect of life, is the source, often, of life's deepest tragedy. Two homely stories illustrate both the insanity of over-attachment to loved ones and the wisdom typical of Buddhist spirit—profound to those who believe in being realistic, cruel to those finding refuge in sentimentality: Reconstructed here from memory, the first story is about a grandmother relentlessly grieving the loss of her dearest grandchild. Having heard astounding reports about Gotama, she came to him for help in restoring her precious child to life. Without directly chiding her, Gotama inquired of her whether she would like to have more such darling children and grandchildren, as many, for example, as there are people in the whole village? Yes, of course, she answered.

But will they not all have to die some day, one at a time?
Yes. Would you not grieve at the death of each one as you
do of this one? Yes. Then would you not have a hundred
grievings, a whole life full of grieving, whereas now you
have only one? Yes. Then are you not really quite well off?
The report has it that the woman went away comforted.
The second story is about a mustard seed. When a woman
whose only son had died, believing her loss unjust beyond
comparison, came to Gotama wanting his life restored, he
said: I shall restore your boy if you will but get me a mustard
seed from a house where no one has died. She searched and
searched and searched and found none in all the homes in
all the villages. She found in the process of her searching,
however, that her grief was a very common one. She too,
having become a little more realistic, was comforted into
accepting her fate as not unjust.

Sensuous pleasures can captivate, enslave and condemn
a life to gnawing hankering. 'There are forms of which sight
is conscious, sounds of which hearing is conscious, odours
of which smell is conscious, savours of which taste is conscious, impressions of which touch is conscious, and mental
objects of which the mind is conscious—all of them bound
up with lusts and exciting to passion. If an almsman hails
and welcomes any of these and cleaves to them, delight will
thus arise in him; and from the beginning of delight, say I,
comes the beginning of Ill. But if he does not hail and
welcome and cleave to them, delight will thus cease in him;
and from the cessation of delight, say I, comes the cessation
of Ill.' (*Further Dialogues of the Buddha*, Vol. II, p. 307.)
Therefore: 'Grow like unto the earth, Rahula; for, as you do
so, no sensory impressions, agreeable or disagreeable, will
grip hold of your heart and stick there. Just as men cast
on the earth's surface things clean and things unclean,

ordure, urine, spittle, pus and gore, and yet the earth is not troubled thereby nor moved to disgust and loathing, even so should you grow like unto the earth; for, as you do so, no sensory impressions, agreeable or disagreeable, will lay hold on your heart and stick there.' (*Further Dialogues of the Buddha*, Vol. I, p. 302.) 'Just as on the earth they cast things, clean and foul, . . . even so, like the earth, I abide with heart, large, abundant, measureless, feeling no hatred, nor ill-will.' (*The Book of the Gradual Sayings*, Vol IV, p. 249.)

Ideas, things of the mind to which one may become attached, are multifarious, ranging from the highest ideal-isms to basest pessimisms, compelling needless self-sacrifice both to mistakenly noble causes and to haunting night-marish phobias. Ideas we will have; and the desire to have ideas, i.e., those which we can experience, use, enjoy and then forget, need yield no harm. But craving for ideas, no matter what form it takes (*See* Ch. 9), can be as crippling as any. 'Regarding that which does not exist..., might there not be anxiety about something objective that does not exist? There might be. . . . But, Lord, might there be anxiety about something subjective that does not exist?' (*The Middle Length Sayings*, Vol. I, p. 175.) Yes. But 'It is the fool who is haunted by fears, dread of dangers, oppres-sion of mind, not the wise man.' (*The Book of the Gradual Sayings*, Vol. I, p. 87.)

Gotama's theory of craving, as interpreted here, amounts in summary to this: accept things as they are, or are going to be (i.e., in all tenses of the verb 'to be', or, indeed, of any verb). Fighting against the inevitable is foolish. Desiring the unattainable is absurd. He did not say stop desiring. He said stop craving. Craving is desiring to excess. Excess desire is any desire, kind or degree, for more than you will get. The greater the disparity between what is desired (greater in whatever way, e.g., in intensity, duration, or quantity) and what will be attained, the greater the frustration, misery, suffering. Since, however, it is difficult in practice for the desirer to detect when his desire tends to excess, what shall he do, what rule can he follow? No rule of thumb is possible except, perhaps, 'when in doubt, don't'. The rule, stop all desiring, which some suggest, is neither wise nor practical. It is unwise, for all satisfaction, all 'profit', all value, all happiness, would disappear with it. It is impractical, for living beings cannot and will not stop desiring; and continued desiring, even some craving, is a part of what one must accept if he is willing to accept things as they are.

Two aids, or two rules, if they can be called rules, pertain to alertness and aloofness. One can be sure that his desire runs not to excess only if he constantly attends alertly to this danger, like one who, having been robbed time and again previously, expectantly awaits the return of a thief. There is no substitute for such alertness. But such alertness may be aided by aloofness, i.e., separation from objects tending to tempt us to excesses (e.g., 'a woman's form') and suppression of compulsions already rooted in us (e.g., 'greed for views'). 'Attachment is bondage, aloofness is freedom.' (*The Book of the Kindred Sayings*, Vol. III, p. 45.) Thus far, Gotama's theory is relatively simple, no matter how hard it may seem in practice. But a further, even if not a different, danger lies concealed in unsuspected cleverness of the thief: the desire to be alert and aloof itself tends to run to excess. How can one avoid defeat when one's desire to do what is best turns out to be the very enemy he must seek to conquer? Gotama's answer, to be discussed in the following chapters, is the middle way entailing dialectic. The only way to catch a dialectical thief is by dialectical alertness. But 'When such conditions are fulfilled, then there will be joy, and happiness, and peace, and in continual mindfulness and self-mastery, one will dwell at ease.' (*Dialogues of the Buddha*, Part I, p. 261.)

6

THE MIDDLE WAY

THAT the middle way is Gotama's most significant contribution to philosophy is a fundamental part of the thesis of this book. Hence the foregoing discussion of desire and craving may be considered preliminary. It is preliminary, however, in the sense of being prior, as a foundation is preliminary to a building. The middle way is built upon desire, is a way among desires, is itself the most ultimate achievable goal of desire. Gotama's middle way exists nowhere else than in the realm of desires, and all satisfied desires, even those which are 'completely satisfied', must be middle-wayed, for to be completely satisfied a desire must have been a desire for neither more nor less satisfaction than was to be achieved. Gotama's middle way is subtle, not only because it is entailed in dialectic, but because it involves certain ambiguities, not merely verbal or etymological, but psychological or actual. The chief purpose of the present chapter is to recognize the significance of these ambiguities (discussed also in Chs. 7 and 8) for interpreting his principle. They will be reviewed, not so that they may be rejected, but so their contribution to the nature of the middle way may be understood and evaluated.

First, the middle way refers to the conclusion reached by Gotama after seven years of exhausting search: avoid both the extremes of debauchery and mortification. The record reports his 'first sermon' as saying: 'These two (dead) ends (*anta*), monks, should not be followed by one who has gone forth. Which two? That which is among sense-pleasures, addiction to attractive sense pleasures, low, of the villager (boorish), of the average man, unariyan, not connected with the goal; and that which is addiction to self-torment, ill, unariyan, not connected with the goal. Now, monks, without adopting either of these two (dead) ends, there is a middle course, fully awakened by the Truthfinder, making for vision, making for knowledge, which conduces to calming, to super-knowledge, to awakening, to *nirvana*.' (*The Book of the Discipline*, Part IV, p. 15. *See also The Book of the Kindred Sayings*, Vol. IV, p. 235, and Vol. V, pp. 356–7.)

Although when seen in perspective the conclusion, avoid extremes, seems clear and obvious, to the person immersed in the problem of seeking particular satisfactions the natural course of events is often unforeseeable. To one who desires, the only course apparent is to seek satisfaction. If he is frustrated, his natural response is to put forth more effort, and more effort takes the form of stronger desire. But the experience of each individual tends to reproduce the experience of mankind, that the stronger the desire the more bitter the frustration. Responding to such bitterness with still stronger desire brings one ultimately to bitterness which he cannot endure. He may then rebel against the very desires themselves which bring him to such bitterness. It is natural, under such circumstances, to turn round and go in the opposite direction. The simple inference, if desire brings frustration, then to stop frustration stop desiring, is apparently irresistible. It was drawn by Gotama's teachers (asceticism was already regarded as ancient wisdom in his time), by Gotama himself (he abandoned a kingdom to pursue asceticism), by his hearers and, after he departed, by followers who made the same mistake, and in his name.

But it is to Gotama's credit that he went far enough to experience the error for himself; the irresistible inference is not so simple, for it entails, paradoxically, a double difficulty: extinction of desire entails extinction of life and the desire to extinguish desire remains a desire. A next natural inference is that life is necessarily tragic, or doubly tragic: not only does desire which is frustrated lead to greater desire and greater frustration until desire itself is unbearable, but also the attempt to escape desire, when frustrated, results in redoubled efforts to escape which may too then become unendurable. Then, except for those seemingly fortunate ones who die from exhaustion, one has to choose, or his temperament chooses for him, between two alternatives: either he responds with a final violent act of will (tantrum) which must either have its way or destroy itself, or with a final surrender of will to acceptance of fate, of whatever good, bad, or indifferent, may come. Surprisingly (for this cannot be inferred from previous experience when it happens for a first time), this very act of being willing to accept what comes, of desiring what one is going to get, brings an unexpected degree of satisfaction—a genuine degree of genuine satisfaction—which, as it then appears, turns out to be the kind of satisfaction sought in the first place. It was this discovery, formulated as a general principle of middle-wayedness, which constituted Gotama's enlightenment.[4]

[4] This discovery is open to every one caught in the toils of desiring who has the ability to observe what is happening (an ability so rare that some Christians conceive it as given by a special act of grace by God). One has, in Jesus' language, to lose his life in order to save it, or, in Calvin's language, to surrender utterly his will to the will of God in order to deserve election. If Jesus' conclusions are interpreted as only for social situations (e.g., desire to do to others as you desire them to do to you), and if Gotama's conclusions are interpreted as for all desire situations, social or otherwise, then Gotama's conclusions will be seen as more general or more universal, and hence more philosophical, in this sense.

Discovery of the principle as a principle is not enough, usually, to

The drawing of further inferences and the actual experiencing of their consequences, i.e., that the desire to stop desiring and the desire to stop the desire to stop desiring, constituting dialectical levels of desires to be calmed by levels of willingness to accept them for what they are even as dialectical, apparently were then achieved by Gotama in the spirit of his enlightenment. Not only during the various 'watches of the night' and the succeeding days, but throughout his lifetime, he strove to realize, i.e., both to comprehend and embody, this enlightenment. The amazingness of his discovery, its contrariness to surface-level common

establish it as a habit. Each new desire, arising seemingly of its own accord, may lead one again through maze-like struggles with hope and defeat, until misery becomes great enough to repeat the lesson in another life-crisis. Backsliding is a normal trait. If Gotama's historic insight was powerful enough to last him a lifetime, it was indeed an astounding achievement and worthy of worship as an event of cosmic significance. But most people apparently must re-experience such insight repeatedly before becoming permanently convinced. If tragedy ends unexpectedly in satisfaction often enough, one may begin to expect the unexpected, and to trust in paradox. The ideal goal then becomes one of habitual and automatic willingness to accept what one is going to get. This willingness is not just a simple surface willingness, but is deep enough to be willing to be unwilling and to accept the consequences of such unwillingness. When the deeper, and especially the deepest, including dialectical depths, levels of desire are satisfied by such willingness, then one can brave the stormiest tempest of surface-level desires and frustrations and still retain profound serenity. Faith, however achieved, that one will get all that he deserves, or that, no matter what happens to him, his is the best of all possible worlds for him, is the cornerstone of such serenity. *Nirvana* is a consciousness of confidence that what is (in all tenses of 'is') is right. Nirvana is enjoyment of an unruffled conviction that no matter what conflicts are experienced they are precisely what one would have chosen for himself if he had planned them omnisciently and omnibenevolently. *Nirvana* is freedom, not necessarily from surface conflict, but from conscience—yet not wholly from conscience, for one will be neither conscience-stricken nor conscience-dulled—but from craving conscientiousness. Conscience is concerned with effort to reach an unreached goal. *Nirvana* is a goal already achieved. Conscientiousness is present when one, still in some doubt about his ability to fulfil, desires to do his duty, however conceived; but having arrived in *nirvana*, one does his duty unconscientiously, confidently, habitually, automatically, freely, because he himself is already wholly committed to accepting it as just what he most wants to do. The ideal man, embodying enlightenment habitually, is called by varying names in different cultures: saint, sage, yogin, rogue, bodhisattva, and wholesome personality. He must, of course, be willing to be misunderstood and be condemned, justly and unjustly, as much as he is so misunderstood and condemned.

sense, and its obvious unbelievability to those who have not experienced the anguish and paradoxical release from anguish for themselves, at first discouraged him from teaching others. Yet such good news was too good to keep, especially from those fellow-strugglers with whom he had shared his efforts for so long. When he revealed his victory to them, they marvelled at his wisdom, and told others who marvelled too. As many came to inquire about his experience, he automatically thereby became their teacher.

In the spirit of the middle way, he accepted his role as a teacher, seeking to be neither more of a teacher nor less of a teacher, nor to be understood as a teacher neither more nor less, than he was to be, and be understood. He not only 'consented by silence' (Cf. *The Book of the Discipline*, Part IV, pp. 291, 297, 316, 324, 355, 488, etc.) to invitations to future dinner-discussion requests but also consented by speaking when circumstances so demanded. He spoke in different ways to suit the needs of varying occasions, but many heard him or about him in contexts conducive to misunderstanding.

He was interpreted, for example, as repudiating asceticism. This he did, but not asceticism as such but only that asceticism which was not in conformity with the middle way. Kassapa, a naked ascetic, once approached him saying: 'I have heard it said, O Gotama, thus: "The Samana Gotama disparages all penance; verily he reviles and finds fault with every ascetic, with every one who lives a hard life." Now those who say this, were they therein repeating Gotama's words, and not reporting him falsely?' Gotama replied: 'No, Kassapa. Those who said so were not following my words. . . .' (*Dialogues of the Buddha*, Part I, pp. 223, 224.) Again: 'Is it true, as it is said, that Gotama the recluse blames all ascetic ways, that he downright upbraids and reproaches every ascetic who lives the hard life?' 'No indeed, sirs, the Exalted One blames not all ascetic ways, nor does he downright upbraid and reproach every ascetic who lives the hard life. The Exalted One blames the blame-worthy, praises the praiseworthy. In doing so the Exalted One is a particularizer; the Exalted One is not one who makes sweeping assertions herein.' 'Indeed, I say not that all ascetic ways are to be pursued. Yet I do not say that all ascetic ways are not to be pursued. I say not that every undertaking, that every effort in training, should be under-taken and made. Yet I do not say the opposite. I say not that every renunciation should be made, nor yet that it should not be made. I say not that every form of release is to be regarded as such, nor yet that it should not be so regarded. If in one practising austerities unprofitable states wax and profitable states wane, such austerity should not be prac-tised.' (*The Book of the Gradual Sayings*, Vol. V, pp. 131–2.'

The middle way avoids extremes, yet it does not ex-tremely avoid extremes. If there are times when one needs to be ascetic, then let him be ascetic; if at times one should rejoice unrestrainedly, let him so rejoice. But it is foolish to desire to legislate either 'Always be ascetic' or 'Always rejoice' when such cannot be law of life. When it gets dark, one should light a lamp if he needs to see. But the need for a lamp ceases at daybreak. He who would follow the rule, 'light the lamp' both night and day is a foolish extremist. And he who desires the lamp put out, not only in daytime but both day and night, follows an opposite folly. The middle way is an extension of the principle, accept things as they are, to both of each pair of opposing directions. It is a principle for adapting to naturally recurring oppositions by achieving a predisposed willingness to accept each in turn for what it is. When 'it occurred to these monks: "Now, when should the rains be entered upon?" They told this matter to the Lord. He said: "I allow (suggest to) you, monks, to enter upon the rains in the rainy season. . . .' 'Now at that time King Seniya Bimbisara of Magadha, desiring to postpone the rains, sent a messenger to the monks, saying: "What if the masters could enter upon the rains at the next full-moon day?" They told this matter to the Lord. He said: "I allow (suggest to) you, monks, to obey kings.' (*The Book of the Discipline*, Part IV, pp. 183–5.)

Secondly, the term 'middle way' refers not merely to a mean between princely debauchery and ascetic mortification but, as we have already begun to indicate, a mediation between all (psychological) opposites. When a young convert, Sona Kolivisa, paced up and down so energetically that his feet bled 'as though there has been a slaughter of cattle', Gotama inquired: 'Were you clever at the lute's stringed music when formerly you were a householder?' 'Yes, Lord.' 'What do you think about this, Sona? When the strings of your lute were too taut, was your lute at that time tuneful and fit for playing?' 'No, indeed, Lord.' 'What do you think about this, Sona? When the strings of your lute were too slack, was your lute at that time tuneful and fit for playing?' 'No, indeed, Lord.' 'What do you think about this, Sona? When the strings of your lute were neither too taut nor too slack, but were keyed to an even pitch, was your lute at that time tuneful and fit for playing?' 'Yes, Lord.' 'Even so, Sona, does too much output of energy conduce to restlessness, does too feeble energy conduce to slothfulness. Therefore do you, Sona, determine upon evenness (*samatam*) in energy and pierce the evenness of the faculties and reflect upon it.' (*The Book of the Discipline*,

Part IV, pp. 239–41. *See also The Book of the Gradual Sayings*, Vol III, p. 267.)

Inherent in Gotama's enlightenment is the doctrine that the law of excluded middle does not hold between opposites. Followers of his middle way do not insist upon the choice: 'either, or, but not both'. They embody a willingness to treat each of two opposites equally, in so far as they are equal as opposites, and unequally, in so far as they are unequal as opposites. Equality is illustrated in the case of a householder who wondered how he should apportion his gift of food to two groups of disputing monks: 'Give gifts to both sides; having given gifts to both sides, hear *dhamma* on both sides; having heard *dhamma* on both sides, choose the views and the approval and the persuasion and the creed of those who are the speakers of the *dhamma*.' (*The Book of the Discipline*, Part IV, p. 508.) Inequality is illustrated by the extremes to which Gotama was reported as willing to go in refraining from condeming Devadatta for his unpardonable behaviour: 'So long, Ananda, as I saw a bright spot in Devadatta, even the prick-end of a horse-hair in size, I declared not: "Devadatta is . . . unpardonable"—but it was when I saw none, that I declared thus. . . .Wouldst thou hear, Ananda, the Tathagata analysing the feelings and thought of man? . . . Suppose . . . I know this of some person: "There is both good and evil in him." Then presently . . . I know: "The good has disappeared, the evil is uppermost; but the root of goodness is not cut off and from that good will proceed. Thus in the future he is bound not to fail." ' (*The Book of the Gradual Sayings*, Vol. III, pp. 287–8.) Opposites tend to be rooted in each other. Even though sunset is sure to be followed by darkness, a seeming total extinction, yet sunrise and midday are also bound to follow. But such recurrence remains uncertain. A seed, if it remains good, will grow in good soil, but if not, then not. Coals, even if blazing, when thrown on stony ground, die out, but when thrown on dry grass, blaze up. Since opposites may be unequal as well as equal, one who is willing to accept things as they are should be willing to treat them as unequal in whatever way they are unequal.

Thirdly, the middle way is not merely a way to the goal but is, in a fundamental sense, the goal itself. Not only is one involved in opposites in variable processes, but the way is not a way beyond opposition or beyond process, but is a way to find the goal within, or as, opposition and process. The goal is middle-wayedness, and middle-wayedness is the goal. One who is willing to accept things as they are can find his goal present in the very searching itself, provided his willingness is deep and genuine. The goal is not something to be extinguished, but something to be realized—'in this very life', now, and without necessary reference to the future. He who projects the goal of life into the future has not reached his goal, looks elsewhere than in the present for it, and demands a future life, or perhaps many future lives, in which to achieve it. But achievement now requires a willingness to accept the actual now, however much complicated and disturbed by tensions of opposing pulls between past and future, hope and fear, satisfaction and frustration, assurance and uncertainty. When one can enjoy life's tensions untensely (including untensely enjoying such tension as is present in this 'tensions untensely'), he has arrived in *nirvana*.

The paradox of seeking to enjoy the very desire for future satisfaction as the goal itself, rather than a future goal which may never be realized, may be seen in a conversation between Maha-Kotthita and Sariputta: 'How is it, reverend Sariputta? Does one live the (good) life under the Exalted

One in the hope: "May I experience in the future just the same thing as I experience here now?"' 'No, indeed, reverend sir.' 'But . . . Sariputta, is it just the reverse of this . . . ?' 'No. . . .' 'Is it then the converse?' 'No. . . .' 'Is it in the hope of avoiding the experience of deeds that have ripened?' 'No. . . .' 'Is it in the hope of experiencing deeds not yet ripe?' 'No. . . .' 'Is it in the hope of experiencing as a trifle, what is serious?' 'No. . . .' 'Is it then the converse?' 'No. . . .' 'Is it in the hope of avoiding the experience of what must be experienced?' 'No. . . .' 'Then is it the converse?' 'No. . . .' 'Reverend Sariputta, to each of the foregoing questions you have replied "No, indeed, reverend sir." What then is the reason that the (good) life is lived under the Exalted One?' (*The Book of the Gradual Sayings*, Vol. IV, pp. 255-6.) The reason is that one may discover for himself that *nirvana*, freedom from attachment, consists in a willingness to find in the midst—the middle way, as ambiguous, confused, complicated, and impermanent as it is—of present tensions the very goal one seeks. Life's problem, 'ill, origin of ill, ending of ill', is ever-present; but its solution is also ever-available. *Nirvana* is not a kind of extinction which is merely negative. Gotama was no nihilist. 'Nay, sir. . . . The Exalted One has thus defined: "This is good; that is bad." By this defining good and bad the Exalted One is a definer. He is no nihilist, not one who defines nothing as certain.' (*The Book of the Gradual Sayings*, Vol. V, p. 131.) *Nirvana* is extinction only of the tendency to want things to be other than they are. This is the ultimate meaning of equanimity.

Further details regarding the interrelations of *nirvana* as middle-wayedness to the eight-fold path and to the *jhanas* are elaborated in the next two chapters.

7

NIRVANA

NIRVANA (*nibbana*) has been described variously, often as indescribable. Each philosopher, Hindu or Buddhist, has had to give some account of it in terms of his presuppositions. Each different set of presuppositions has somewhat different implications regarding its nature. Yet all of them conceive it as a goal, even if, at times, as quite independent of its being aimed at. All conceive it as quiescent, if not completely, then at least essentially. It is commonly thought to be arrived at by cessation of something, whether of craving, desire, individual existence, or all movement. Gotama, as interpreted here, conceived its achievement as through extinction, not of all desire, but of desire to have things different from the way they are. Hence *nirvana* consists in middle-wayedness in the complicated sense developed in the previous and following chapters. Attention here will be focused upon *nirvana* as equanimity, represented by the Sanskrit and Pali stem *sam*, and upon what appear to be garbled reports of Gotama's view as transformed through transmitting thought-systems which seem to be somewhat at variance with his.

The stem, *sam*, with its variants and derivatives, obviously has had a long and complicated history. For example, in Sanskrit (Cf. M. Monier-Williams, *A Sanskrit-English Dictionary*, Oxford University Press, London, 1899), *śam* (pp. 1053–4), *sam* (pp. 1111–34, 1141–8), *sam* (pp. 1152–81), and *sām* (pp. 1197, 1205–7), mean, singly and collectively, withness, togetherness, conjunction, union; likeness, similarity, sameness; equality, equilibrium, balance, equipoise; evenness, smoothness, constancy, calmness, peacefulness, tranquillity; allayment, satisfaction, completion, perfection. In Pali (Cf. T. W. Rhys Davids and Wm. Stede, *Pali-English Dictionary*, Part VIII, Pali Text Society, London, 1925, 1949), *san* and its variations (pp. 114–18, 121–6, 128–31, 134–8) mean one and the same, even, at one, together, towards one point, implying conjunction and completeness, and *sam* and its variations (pp. 140–6, 163–4) mean calmness, tranquillity; like, equal, same; impartial, upright, of even mind. In English, the word 'same', which is etymologically related to the foregoing, still ambiguously connotes both a togetherness, likeness, equality, union of two (or more) things and an evenness, undisturbedness, continuity, identity, wholeness of one.

Another fundamental ambiguity, pertaining to means and end or to way and goal, mentioned previously, is inherent also in *sam*. *Sam* refers to a way, a middle way, an even way, a smooth way; it refers also to a goal, an end of action, a termination of striving, a pacification of motion, a completion of endeavour, a perfection of tendency. *Nirvana* consists in equanimity and equanimity embodies an ambiguity of way and goal—the way is the goal and the goal is the way. *Sam* means sameness of way and goal in the ambiguous sense just described: a togetherness, equality, union of way and goal as two, and an evenness, continuity, identity, wholeness of that one which is both way and goal. Intellect may distinguish, but life cannot separate, way and goal. To have smoothed the way is to have achieved the goal; to have achieved the goal is to be going smoothly on life's way. To have achieved a willingness to accept things as they are is thus both a way and a goal. This constitutes *bodhi* (enlightenment), and one who so achieves, by both knowing and living, *bodhi* thereby becomes a *bodhisattva*.

The significance of Gotama's doctrine—and his revolt, if such it was, from the teachings of his inherited tradition—may be found in the contrast between 'Samanas and Brahmanas, as Samana-ship and Brahman-ship.' (*Dialogues of the Buddha*, Part I, p. 227. *See also* pp. 229, 232, 234, 235.) Did not the Brahman view of *nirvana* consist in perfect and undisturbed equilibrium of the three *gunas* (*rajas*, *sattva*, and *tamas*), a complete cessation of all life, whereas Gotama found the goal to be, not beyond life, not through a stilling of life, but a stillness in life, i.e., in one's accepting life as he finds it?

Likewise, the term *sambhodi* is 'of first importance in the history of Buddhism'. (T. W. Rhys Davids, *Dialogues of the Buddha*, Part I, p. 191.) As if to counteract the influence of interpretations of Gotama's enlightenment as indicating a step-wise way to extinction as a goal, the term *sam* was added to *bodhi* to give emphasis to the kind of enlightenment intended.

Sam is the name for the middle way, the way-goal, *nirvana*. It is not a mere, narrow, or exclusive middle (*madhya*), but a broad, ambiguous, inclusive middle (*sam*). Each step of the eight-fold path, which may well have existed before the time of Gotama, was interpreted, or re-interpreted, in terms of *sam*. The very ambiguities involved in *sam*, discussed above (pp. 43–44 and Ch. 6) and below (Ch. 8), were intended to be present in the interpretation of each step. *Sam*, as the universal principle of accepting things as they are, applies to everything, including each step one takes in any step-wise plan. *Sam* is equanimity, and each step should be taken with, and enjoyed through, equanimity. The steps, in Sanskrit, in Pali, and their usual mistranslations into English, respectively, are as follows: *samyagdrsti*, *sammaditthi*, right views (beliefs); *samyak-sankalpa*, *sammasankappa*, right resolve (thoughts); *sam-yagvak*, *sammavaca*, right speech; *samyakkarmanta*, *sam-makammanta*, right conduct (acts); *samyagajiva*, *samma-ajiva*, right livelihood; *samyagvyayama*, *sammavayama*, right effort (endeavour); *samyaksmrti*, *sammasati*, right mindfulness; *samyaksamadhi*, *sammasamadhi*, right concen-tration. (Cf. S. C. Chatterjee and D. M. Datta, *An Introduc-tion to Indian Philosophy*, pp. 129–34. University of Calcutta, Calcutta, 1939, 1954.)

The term 'right', although fitting better into the puri-tanic, rigoristic, and perfectionistic preconceptions of many Western translators, and into the perfectionistic (extinction-istic) tendencies of Theravada, is only slightly justified. The writer cannot wholly agree with Mohan Singh, who inspired this study, when he sees 'absolutely no justification for . . . the use of right for the *sam* which is prefixed to these eight . *(New Light on Buddha's First Sermon*, p. 7. Academy of Spiritual Culture, Elephanta, Dhera Dun, India, 1949.) There is some justification, though it is very little. Right action is that which is intended to result in the best. *Sam* is the best. Hence *sam* action is right action. The translation is justified. However, right, in Western thought, tends to be rigorously opposed to wrong, and rectitude has a stiff-backed, resolute, insistent, demanding quality about it; right and wrong too often are conceived as divided by the law of excluded middle. But in *sam* the principle of excluded middle is, if not entirely missing, subordinated to the principle of the middle way. Gotama opposed both of two opposites, by not taking sides; his was not a violent opposition, but an opposition to violence; and his was not an exclusive opposition, but an opposition to exclusiveness. To represent Gotama's message as taking sides, i.e., as siding with the right as against the wrong, is to misrepresent it. Wrongness, when present, consists in taking sides, e.g., either of debauchery or mortification, or of desirousness or the extinction of desire. Wrongness consists in attachment —attachment to either side, and any system which divides things into two groups, the right and the wrong, recommending attachment to the right and avoidance (negative attachment) to the wrong, is itself a wrong system, a system which fails to comprehend *sam*. *Sam* is antithetical to right conceived as opposed to wrong. Hence the translation is not justified.

Sam does not exclude side-taking absolutely, however. In life, actually one may have to take sides, but he should do so with neither avidity nor aversion. Since one should want to do what he has to do, including taking sides on occasion, he will not run away from side-taking, but he will keep divisive issues at the surface of his life, if possible, and not waste his life by devoting it to unreal issues. The real issue is: can you take it as it comes?

The eight-fold path is not to be interpreted, as is so often claimed, as a series of negative precepts—avoidances, renunciations, abstinences, extinctions—but as a reminder that at each step, for those who proceed by steps, there is a goal to be found. Let us examine each of the eight steps in turn:

Right view, or belief, or 'outlook is to know Ill, the origin of Ill, the cessation of Ill, and the path that leads to the cessation of Ill'. (*Further Dialogues of the Buddha*, Vol. II, p. 298.) Once one has grasped the basic principle, desire for what will not be attained ends in frustration, he already has all that is needed in the way of belief. He does not need to look elsewhere, into theories of the origin and nature of the universe and man, in order to have right view. Accepting this principle gives one a proper perspective regarding all problems. In believing that one must accept things as they are, he is already accepting things as they are, relative to this belief. Right view is to have achieved a sense of equanimity, of confidence that what is is right and that what one believes is true because he enjoys it without question. But such a view is 'right' not because equanimity is to be measured by some standard of rightness, but because rightness has its ultimate basis for definition in equanimity.

'Right resolves are to resolve to renounce the world and to do no hurt or harm.' (*Ibid.*) Superficially, this means not to kill or injure persons or animals either by physical violence or ill will. Basically, it means willingness to accept the world as it is, for to desire to change it is to want to do violence to it. And such violence ranges all the way from a whimsical wish that it were just a little bit different to an insistence upon changing it completely, as in killing, for example. To want to extinguish anything which will naturally continue, including wanting to extinguish craving altogether, is just such a desire. Right resolve consists in resolving to let come what may, including desires, satisfactions, frustrations, desires to end desires, and desires to change things. Idealists, those who want to make things better, exist, and whether they succeed or fail, their existence, and their success or failure, is a part of what is and is to be accepted. Equanimity, or enjoyment of the realization that this is the best of all possible worlds, regardless of whether it is to be improved or not to be improved, is the ultimate goal of all resolution.

'Right Speech is to abstain from lies and slander, from

reviling and from tattle.' (*Ibid.*) That these curbs on obvious
ill intent, like those on killing and hurting, are necessary to
social welfare is testified amply by how universally they
occur in human mores. No intention to minimize their
practical need and worth is implied in asserting that they are
simply specific varieties of a more fundamental principle:
any assertion, or willingness to assert, that things are, or
should be, other than they are, or are going to be other than
they are, is a lie. Unwillingness to accept things as they are
is the basis of lying, and any expression of that unwillingness is wrong speech. Perhaps, at this point, the reader may
wish a reminder that the 'is' or 'are' in 'things as they are'
includes not only all tenses of the verb 'to be' but of all
verbs. The existence of which Gotama spoke includes past,
present, and future, in this and, if any, other worlds. To
want the past to have been different, and to say that it was
different from what it was, is to lie as truly as to wish the
present or future to be different from what it is or will be.
The principle holds also for conditional and subjunctive
tenses—might, could, would, should be or have been—but
these are, at best, secondary tenses implying a wistfulness, a
degree of wishing, that things might, could, would, or
should be different than they are. Those who dwell much
with them manifest not intuitive enjoyment of present
assurance, but a spirit of dissatisfaction and frustration.
They are tenses especially suited for more subtle lying. A
person who overtly refuses to lie bluntly may nevertheless
deceive himself into believing that he is not lying when he
is. May not all assertions in such tenses be reduced to the
implied general lie: if the world were only different from
what it is, then I would be happy? *Sambhodi* is living in the
realization that what is cannot be and should not be other
than it is, and *sammavaca* is saying so, not merely through

specific assertorical sentences, but through the entire expression of one's life in enjoying it for what it is. Superficially, a liar may deceive others without deceiving himself, but basically, the liar deceives, if not only, at least first of all, himself. Unhappiness, or anguish, automatically results from basic lying, and *sammavaca* automatically releases one from anguish due to such lying.

'Right acts are to abstain from taking life, from stealing, from lechery.' (*Ibid.*) Looking beneath these common immoralities to a more fundamental meaning of *samyakkarmanta* (*karma-anta* means end of *karma*), we find recommended a giving up of moral calculativeness, desire for rewards, and interest in choosing between alternatives, in favour of profound appreciation of the actual as the ideal. Since sooner or later, i.e., whenever one arrives at his goal, *nirvana*, he must enjoy it as a goal in order to enjoy it at all, why not now, 'in this very life'? The law of *karma*, or justice, dictates good rewards for good deeds, bad rewards for bad deeds. But does this causal process go on interminably, or is man a goal-seeker, seeking to end *karma* (*karma-anta*) in *nirvana*? Why not let the end come quickly? He who demands justice implies that injustice exists and that, therefore, this is not the best of all possible worlds. He will be forever entangled in righting wrongs, always struggling against evil, always in anguish, always frustrated, always unhappy. If one believes that his happiness depends upon a favourable balance of good karmas, he will be constantly concerned about his fate, his future; and attention to his future competes with enjoyment of the present. One should abstain from stealing from the end of life and giving to the means, or should renounce stealing from the actual present and giving to an uncertain future. He who seeks justice, believing that each man should be rewarded for his own good and bad choices or deeds, tends to believe he is treated unjustly when suffering evils resulting from causes over which he has no control. The ideal of justice justifies regret and revenge, but revenge merely creates greater evil. Only if one is willing to accept the world as it is as the best possible (most just), regardless of whether he is or is not responsible for the consequences, can there be an end of *karma*, of struggle, of anguish. Not justice, but love, is the end of *karma*; not love as attachment to otherness, but love of what is. *Sam* is not mere love of one for another, as of parent for child, which is attached love, but love for what is, attachment to what is in such a way that one does not cling to it after it is gone and replaced by something else which then is. A mother whose child has grown to independent manhood and who still calls him 'My baby', expresses love not so much for what he is as for what he was. This does not mean that we should not appreciate the past for what it is, as past, but that we should not mistake it for the present; nor should we treat the present as if it were already gone, or the future as if it were already here. *Sam* is love of things as they are, no matter how they are. One should, of course, abstain from stealing, but not merely from depriving others of their means. Demanding of the present more justice or more love of or by others than one gets is stealing—stealing from the irreplaceable enjoyment of the present.

'Right livelihood is that by which the disciple of the Noble One supports himself, to the exclusion of wrong modes of livelihood.' (*Ibid.*) Here again, what is usually interpreted according to commonly accepted principles of morality (the now-redundant not kill, not steal, not lie) hides a deeper significance. The English word 'supports' easily suggests specific 'means of support' (hence avoid pro-

fessions of soldier, robber, salesman) but veils the more
general and profound 'whatever is life-giving'—both food
and confidence. Literally, *jiva* means life, and *a-jiva* means
'to, toward, near, as far as' life. It is true that *a-jiva* has a
means-character, a directional significance, about it, but
when modified by *samyak* reveals a means-end quality in
which means and end are fused. *Samyagajiva* is enjoyment
of self-sustaining life in which all means of sustaining life
are accepted as equally essential in bringing it to completion
in and through itself. Equanimity relative to livelihood is as
rewarding, or is as much a reward, as equanimity regarding
views or speech or any other aspect of life. Since one must,
in the world in which he finds himself, earn his livelihood
by whatever physically and socially necessary means are
available, these must be reckoned with as part of what is.
But, although one must eat to live, he does not live to eat.
Life is the end-in-itself, and whoever devotes himself to a
means in a way which distracts him from the end itself is
pursuing a wrong means of livelihood.

'Right endeavour is when an Almsman brings his will
to bear, puts forth endeavour and energy, struggles and
strives with all his heart, to stop bad and wrong qualities
which have not yet arisen from ever arising, to renounce
those which have already arisen, to foster good qualities
which have not yet arisen, and finally to establish, clarify,
multiply, enlarge, develop, and perfect those good qualities
which are there already.' (*Ibid.*) *Vayama*, struggle, effort,
exertion, when modified by *samyak*, is endeavour without
anxiety. Right effort is neither extinction of effort nor effort
for the sake of effort; is neither no effort nor wasted effort.
It is effort enjoyed, not for its own sake as effort, but for
the sake of life lived for its own sake. When appreciated as
the effort wherewith life sustains and realizes itself, then it

achieves a self-contained value. Right endeavour devotes itself not to a means to a means to a means, but to the end. Where means are involved, one should seek the most immediate and direct way to the end. Right effort is effort to keep the end in view, not some distant future end, but the present end. It consists not in seeking rebirth and greater future reward but in exercising constant appreciation in this very life of the end-aspect of what is.

'Right mindfulness is when realizing what the body is, what feelings are, what the heart is, and what the mental states are, the Almsman dwells ardent, alert and mindful, in freedom from wants and discontents attendant on any of these things.' (*Ibid.*) No matter how many things, such as body, feelings, heart, ideas, arouse one's interest, he willingly accepts each for what it is, keeping in mind his sense of equanimity relative to it. Another sutta, attributed to the Exalted One, develops 'the four-fold setting of mindfulness' in some detail. When a person attends to 'body, feeling, thoughts, and ideas, let him so look upon each, that he remains ardent, self-possessed, and mindful, having overcome both the hankering and dejection common in the world'. (*Dialogues of the Buddha*, Part II, p. 327.)

'He keeps on considering how the body is something that comes to be, or ... something that passes away; or ...the coming to be with the passing away; or again, conscious that "There is the body", mindfulness hereof becomes thereby established, far enough for the purposes of knowledge and of self-collectedness.' (*Ibid.*, p. 328.) 'When he is walking (he) is aware of it thus: "I walk"; or when he is standing, or sitting, or lying down, he is aware of it. However he is disposing the body, he is aware thereof.' (*Ibid.*, p. 329.) 'Whether he departs or returns, whether he looks at or looks away from, whether he has drawn in or stretched out (his limbs), whether he has donned under-robe, over-robe, or bowl, whether he is obeying the calls of nature—is aware of what he is about. In going, standing, sitting, sleeping, watching, talking, or keeping silence, he knows what he is doing.' (*Ibid.*, p. 329.)

'When affected by a feeling of pleasure, (he) is aware of it, reflecting: "I feel a pleasurable feeling!" So, too, is he aware when affected by a painful feeling, or by a neutral feeling, or by a pleasant or painful or neutral feeling concerning material things, or by a pleasant or painful or neutral feeling concerning spiritual things.' (*Ibid.*, p. 333.) 'If his thought be lustful, (he) is aware that it is so, or if his thought be free from lust, is aware that it is so; or if his thought be full of hate, or free from hate, or dull, or intelligent, or attentive, or distrait, or exalted, or not exalted, or mediocre, or ideal, or composed, or decomposed, or liberated, or bound, he is aware in each case that his thought is so.' (*Ibid.*, p. 334.) 'As to ideas, (he) continues to consider ideas from the point of view of: sensuous desire, ill-will, sloth and torpor, flurry and worry, and doubt; the six internal and external spheres of sense; and truth, energy, joy, serenity, rapture, equanimity.' (*Ibid.*, pp. 334–6.) When one regards anything, no matter what, with *samyaksmrti*, attention to it with equanimity, a middle way between hankering and dejection, then he 'is aware of it as it really is'. (*Ibid.*, p. 337.)

8

DHYANA

THE eighth fold or step is, for those who interpret the folds as steps, not so much one step as a new flight of steps, four in number, usually, which then ends in a fifth or final step into steplessness. *Sam-a-dhi*, a word with a broad range of meanings, including putting or adhering together, completion, assent, has been explained in terms of *dhyana* (Sanskrit), *jhana* (Pali), *ch'an-na* or *ch'an* (Chinese) and *ẓen* (Japanese), and translated, unsatisfactorily, as concentration, meditation, musing, rapture, ecstasy, and trance.

Each of the four additional steps or stages in extinguishing craving has then to be described: 'Gladness springs up within him on his realizing that (i.e., right mindfulness), and joy arises to him thus gladdened, and so rejoicing all his frame becomes at ease, and being thus at ease he is filled with a sense of peace, and in this peace his heart is stayed. Then estranged from lusts, aloof from evil dispositions, he enters into and remains in the First Rapture—a stage of joy and ease born of detachment, reasoning and investigation going on the while. . . . Then . . . suppressing all reasoning and investigation (he) enters and abides in the Second *Jhana*, a state of joy and ease, born of serenity and concentration, when no reasoning and investigation goes on, . . . a state of elevation of mind, a tranquillization of the heart within. . . . Then . . . holding aloof from joy, (he) becomes equable (*upekhako*, literally "looking on"; imperturbable, impartial, tolerant, unsusceptible, stoical, composed—all of these possible renderings are unsatisfactory); and mindful and self-possessed he experiences that ease which the Arahats talk of when they say: "The man serene and self-possessed is well at ease," and so he enters into and abides in the *third Jhana.* . . . Then . . . by the putting away alike of ease and of pain, by the passing away alike of any elation or dejection he had previously felt, (he) enters into and abides in the *fourth Jhana*, a state of pure self-possession and equanimity, without pain and without ease. . . . With his heart thus serene, made pure, translucent, cultured, devoid of evil, supple, ready to act, firm, and imperturbable, he applies and bends down his mind to that insight that comes from knowledge. He grasps the fact: "This body of mine has form, it is built up of the four elements, it springs from father and mother, it is continually renewed by so much boiled rice and juicy foods, its very nature is impermanence, and it is subject to abrasion, dissolution, and disintegration; and therein is this consciousness of mine, too, bound up, on that does it depend."' (*Dialogues of the Buddha*, Part I, pp. 84–87.)

Various accounts of the *jhanas* in different suttas, although revealing a common core, differ somewhat in detail. For example, in one sutta where Gotama is reported as testifying concerning his own original enlightenment, he says: 'I entered into and abided in the fourth meditation which has neither anguish nor joy and which is entirely purified by equanimity and mindfulness. But yet the pleasurable feeling arising in me, persisted without impinging on my mind.' (*The Middle Length Sayings*, Vol. I, p. 302. For other accounts of *jhanas*, see ibid., pp. 52–3, 246–53, 331–2; *ibid.*, Vol. II, pp. 126–8; *Dialogues of the Buddha*, Part I, pp.

84–6; *ibid.*, Part II, p. 345; *ibid.*, Part III, p. 124; *The Book of the Kindred Sayings*, Vol. IV, pp. 146, 151–4, 179–85; *ibid.*, Vol. V, pp. 9, 187–91, 272, 281–3; *The Book of the Gradual Sayings*, Vol. I, pp. 165–6; *ibid.*, Vol. IV, pp. 294–5.)

'When I have reached such a state, if I walk up and down, at such time my walking is to me celestial. If I stand, at such time my standing is celestial. If I sit, my sitting is to me celestial.' (*The Book of the Gradual Sayings*, Vol. I, p. 166.)

These apparently more direct quotations, idealizing enjoyed vitality, seem at variance with others idealizing extinction not only of desire but also of consciousness: 'By passing beyond the consciousness of form, by putting an end to the sense of resistance, by paying no heed to the idea of distinction, thinking: "The space is infinite," reaches up to and remains in the mental state in which the mind is concerned only with the consciousness of the infinity of space. . . . By passing quite beyond the consciousness of space as infinite . . . and again . . . by passing quite beyond the consciousness of the infinity of cognition, thinking: "There is nothing that really is," reaches up to and remains in the mental state in which the mind is concerned only with the unreality of things. . . . So he falls into trance. Thus is it that the attainment of the cessation of conscious ideas takes place step by step.' (*Dialogues of the Buddha*, Part I, pp. 249–52.)

One version describes the fourth *jhana* as resulting in power to proceed at ease in two directions: free enjoyment of vivid imagination and penetrating insight into the heart of things as they are. First: 'He enjoys (a prosperous imagination)[5] in its various modes—being one he becomes many, or having become many becomes one again; he becomes visible or invisible; he goes, feeling no obstruction,

[5] Rhys Davids translates this as 'Wonderous Gift'.

to the further side of a wall or rampart or hill, as if through
air; he penetrates up and down through solid ground, as if
through water; he walks on water without breaking
through, as if on solid ground. . . .' Second: 'Penetrating
with his own heart the hearts of other beings, of other men,
he knows them. He discerns the passionate to be passionate,
and the calm mind to be calm; the angry mind to be angry,
and the peaceful mind to be peaceful; the dull mind to be
dull, and the alert mind to be alert; . . . the free mind to be
free, and the enslaved mind enslaved. Just as a woman on
considering attentively the image of her own face in a
bright and brilliant mirror . . . would, if it had a mole on it,
know that it had, and if not, would know that it had not.'
(*Dialogues of the Buddha*, Part I, pp. 88–90. *See also The
Middle Length Sayings*, Vol. II, pp 173–5.) For those, like
Kevaddha, who mistakenly believed it worth while to seek
through the higher *jhanas*, mystic power to become invisible or to step through a solid wall, Gotama had a reply:
'It is because I perceive the danger in the practice of mystic
wonders, that I loath, abhor, and am ashamed thereof.'
(*Dialogues of the Buddha*, Part I, p. 278.)

What, then, are the *jhanas*? Something so difficult to
interpret that various schools have disagreed about the
degree and kind of extinction or realization to be achieved
(from total extinction of desire, consciousness, or being, to
realization of self as cosmic perfection through the *bhumi* or
Mahayanic stages of spiritual progress,[6] and to Zen's degree-
lessly sudden enlightenment), leaves the field open for
further speculation. Taking a fresh look, with somewhat
different presuppositions, the writer, viewing the *jhanas* as
degrees or stages of relaxation, joins other interpreters in

[6] *See* N. Dutt, *Aspects of Mahayana Buddhism and its Relation to Hinayana*,
Ch. IV, Luzac and Co., Ltd., London, 1930.

conceiving the way and goal as means and end relative to freedom from anguish—negative as extinction of craving, positive as achievement of *nirvana*. Four emphases of this interpretation may be distinguished, pertaining to generality, means-ends, dialectic, and ambiguity (*sam*); and the four are interrelated.

1. Generality, as conceived here, is of many sorts, all of them concerned with accepting things as they are. One may achieve an attitude of acceptance relative to one thing or kind of thing and fail to do so regarding other things. He may accept himself but not the world, or the world but not himself. He may accept his biological status as a man, but not his social role, or his social role but not his biological status. He may be confident of his hopes for the future, but unhappy with the present, or he may be content with his present but fearful of the future. He may be content with present and future, but despise his ancestry, biological or cultural. Each individual has his own peculiar anxieties, phobias and manias, feelings of inferiority and insecurity. These may range from temporary disturbances caused by particular circumstances to deep-lying disharmonies due to cultural, social, biological, physiological, political, econo-mic, semantic, theological, and even astronomical con-ditions. It is not a purpose of this exposition to try to settle the specific question as to what the ranges and degrees of generality of acceptance may be or should be expected, nor which of the various schools of thought on this subject are closer to the truth, but merely to point out that, relative to each range or degree of generality, however conceived, the problem of accepting or not accepting things as they are recurs. Human happiness requires some way of achieving or re-achieving such willingness relative to each. *Jhanas*, as here conceived, represent an attempt to deal with this

problem. One may well doubt that Gotama fixed the number as four, since 'the four *jhanas* were regarded by the early Buddhists as older than Buddhism'. (T. W. Rhys Davids in *Dialogues of the Buddha*, Part I, p. 51, footnote. For eight in number, *see Further Dialogues of the Buddha*, Vol. II, pp. 7–8.) But that he recognized the problem and sought to deal with it need not be questioned. Part, if not all, of the significance not only of Hindu and Buddhist systems of yoga but also of the main burden of Hindu and Buddhist philosophies is their effort and success in dealing with this problem of increasing ranges of generality.

The specific directions for controlling attention relative to the objects of each of the senses, the channels themselves, memory, imagination, distinctions of self and object, etc., all bear upon the problem. The eight-fold path may be interpreted as a step-wise attempt to achieve increasing generality of acceptance. The four *jhanas*, described above, appear to begin with relatively complete acceptance, yet with 'reasoning and investigation going on all the while', indicating that one is not yet content to accept things so completely that he is willing to stop reasoning about them or investigating them. At another stage, he is willing to cease reasoning and investigating, but not without attention to ease and joy. Finally, one is so willing that he will accept things as they are even without ease or joy. When acceptance reaches complete generality, i.e., reserves no exceptions, then *samadhi* is perfect.

2. It should be noted that this process of increasing acceptance involves a shift in emphasis from means to ends, from being forward-looking, interested in how things are going to be different in the future, to appreciation of the present. The *jhanas* may be interpreted as degrees of shifting from concern about means to enjoyment of ends. Each

new increase in generality of acceptance entails an increase in what is included in that which is experienced as an end. *Jhanas* are degrees of freedom from anxiety. *Jhanas* constitute levels of clarification or enlightenment relative to the extensiveness of the generality embodied in present enjoyment. *Jhanas* are successive degrees of diminution of one's desire to interfere wilfully in the natural course of events. *Jhanas* are shifts of interest increasingly from what ought to be to what is; when *samadhi* is complete, interest in, or awareness of, oughtness has disappeared as completely fulfilled in what is. When the end is realized, the means which ought to be used to reach it become irrelevant. Gotama's parable of the raft—a raft needed to cross the river is discarded when the other shore is reached, not carried about forever after as a burden on one's head—illustrated the point. (Cf. *The Middle Length Sayings*, Vol. I, p. 173.)

3. 'He seems to have thought of experience as genuinely dialectical and paradoxical in character.' (Howard L. Parsons, 'Buddha and Buddhism: A New Appraisal,' *Philosophy East and West*, Vol. I, No. 3, October, 1951, p. 20.) Dialectic is related to generality as one of the most general of the specific varieties of generality. Although at first seeming different from and opposed to generality because it involves negation, including negation of generality, dialectic is really more general than most types of generality because it positively includes both of each pair of opposites. For example, that which includes both all generality and all specificity is more general, because more inclusive, than either all generality or all specificity without the other. Hence dialectic, in this sense, is at once more general than generality, because inclusive of both generality and specificity, and also less general than generality

because, in being general, it remains a variety of generality.

Every concept capable of being interpreted as in some sense completely general entails dialectic. The concept of *jhanas*, as increasingly general degrees or stages of accepting things as they are, is just such a concept. One must, eventually, become *jhanic* about *jhanas*, i.e., be willing to accept *jhanas* as *jhanas*, the number of *jhanas*, whatever it is, for what it is, and the difficulties involved in achieving such willingness for what they are. The difficulties involved in ascending *jhanas* are in part dialectical difficulties, and he who has achieved a willingness to accept life as paradoxical and as dialectical has already prepared himself for more rapid ascent.

In how far Gotama was aware of the intricacies of dialectic is not an issue which will be settled here. But that dialectic was involved in his predicament, that he was aware of dialectical difficulties, and that his principle, including its extension to the middle way, is able to meet the difficulties, need not be doubted. What is the evidence? The very setting in which Gotama's enlightenment occurred and the first, and later, sermons about its central principle reveal his solution as dialectical. 'Let a man neither give himself over to pleasures . . . nor yet let him give himself over to self-mortification. . . . To the exclusion of both these extremes, the Truth-Finder has discovered a middle course. . . .' (*Further Dialogues of the Buddha*, Vol. II, p. 286.) Here one is already involved in dialectic, for in seeking a middle way between desiring and desiring to stop desiring, one then desires to achieve this middle more than he will; hence he needs to stop this dialectical desire and to seek a new middle way between this new level of desiring and desiring to stop desiring.

The eight-fold path may be seen as eight areas in which

the dialectical principle is to be applied. Right view entails, dialectically, right view of right view. The seeming clumsiness and redundancy of the usual formula may be explained as, and taken as evidence for, dialectical intention. The four truths include the eight-fold path, and the eight-fold path, in its first step explicitly and in each step implicitly, includes the four truths. Right resolve entails resolving rightly to rightly resolve. Or equanimous resolve involves equanimously resolving to resolve equanimously. One has to be willing to accept the truth for what it is or he will be having a false view of truth. Right speech must be spoken about rightly or error will result; one should speak equanimously about equanimous speech or he will be refuting himself. Right action is accepting things as they are and, dialectically, to act rightly, one has to accept 'right action as accepting things as they are'. Not only are injury, assault and theft wrong, but there are wrong ways of injuring, assaulting and thieving. 'There is non-harming for a harmful individual to go by; there is restraint from onslaught for an individual to go by who makes onslaught on creatures; there is restraint from taking what is not given for an individual who is a taker of what is not given.' (*The Middle Length Sayings*, Vol. I, p. 55.) A discontented murderer, one who wishes he had killed more violently, is worse than one who accepts the violence actually done as just what he wanted. Right livelihood is life living itself, for itself, not for something else; the more you search for the purpose of life, the more you find it in the way life lives itself (including living itself as a search for its own purpose in living). Right endeavour entails endeavouring rightly to rightly endeavour; the endeavour to be freed from anxiety itself needs to be unanxious endeavour. Right mindfulness entails right mindfulness about right mindfulness; it is awareness

of things (phenomena) as they really are, including awareness of mindfulness as it really is.

The eighth fold, *samma-samadhi*, is the most obviously
dialectical of all. Not only is *a-dhi* modified by *sam*, togetherness conditioned by equanimity, but *sam-adhi* is
modified by *samma*; equanimity of togetherness is itself
conditioned by equanimity, a higher or deeper or more
equanimous equanimity. The usual exposition of *samadhi*
reveals it to be not so much a terminus to the eight-fold
path, an absolute finality, as the beginning of a new series,
or a new dimension of dialectical levels. It appears, thus, as
a terminus which is not a terminus. And its new series of
jhanas, dialectical levels in themselves, terminates in a fourth
or fifth *jhana* which also is a terminus which is not a terminus, but a transition to a new dimension described in
terms of awareness of 'the sphere of infinite space . . . of
infinite consciousness . . . of nothingness . . . of neither
perception nor non-perception. . . .' (*The Book of the
Gradual Sayings*, Vol. IV, p. 295.)

Dialectical processes do not stop with 'neither perception nor non-perception' but go on to the 'principle of
four-cornered negation' (Cf. 'The Principle of Four-
Cornered Negation in Indian Philosophy', P. T. Raju,
Review of Metaphysics, June, 1954, pp. 694–713), which
may be stated, for example, as a condition which is neither
perception, nor non-perception, nor both perception and
non-perception, nor neither perception nor non-perception.
Now must one not conclude that this conception, recorded
many times in the Pali texts, could not have been reached
without great dialectical endeavour and astuteness? Any
inference regarding in how far Gotama himself indulged in
such dialectical extremes will have to square itself with
certain facts: his principle and its dialectical extension as the

middle way was sufficient to imply and to stimulate the required inferences; his own rejection of 'greed for views' (*see* Ch. 9) implies disinterest in (at least no craving for) carrying dialectic to dialectical extremes; his willingness, in accepting things as they are, to accept them as dialectical, as having dialectical extremes, and as including as normal the failure to avoid extremes.

Turning, or returning, to the *jhanas* as levels of acceptance of things as they are, one may see dialectical intent in each of the four *jhanas* even as traditionally interpreted. For example, the first *jhana* is described as 'a state of joy and ease born of detachment, reasoning and investigating going on the while'. (*See* pp. 92, 97.) To be detached from all things, and yet attached to reasoning about and investigating those things, or even about such detachment, requires a further, opposite, and still more general, type of detachment, a higher *jhana*. The second *jhana*, 'when no reasoning and investigation goes on', is 'a state of joy and ease'. But here the danger of attachment to joy and ease needs to be overcome by a willingness to accept things as they are, without joy and ease, which then appears as the third *jhana*. But this willingness to accept things as they are without joy and ease retains a trace of 'one-sided concentration'. (*Dialogues of the Buddha*, Part I, p. 200.) In the fourth and final *jhana*, one is so completely willing to accept things as they are that he is willing to accept them with or without joy and ease, with or without frustration, with or without equanimity, with or without dialectic, with or without *jhanas*, even with or without (other) acceptance. In this state of willingness, distinction between the actual and the possible is difficult to maintain, for to be attached to this distinction entails more attachment than exists in the fourth, or even any, *jhana*.

In the fourth *jhana*, 'anything is possible', meaning that, regardless of what appears or how it appears, one's willingness to accept it for what it is is already precommitted. Does this mean that one has the power to travel 'cross-legged in the sky, like birds on wing'? (*Dialogues of the Buddha*, Part I, p. 89.) No. It intends to be a most realistic view, accepting, without exception, each thing for what it is, a dream for a dream, a frustration for a frustration, death for death, without any degree of wanting a dream to be more real than it is, or frustration to be less frustrating than it is, or death, when it comes, to come later or to have come sooner than it does. Then one's walking, or standing, or sitting is 'celestial', for there is no difference between being celestial and being completely realistic when one is wholly willing to accept things as they are. This is *nirvana*, in which the ideal is completely realized through finally reaching complete willingness to accept the actual as the ideal— 'dwelling, here and now, beyond appetites, consummate, unfevered, in bliss, in (wholesomeness)' (*Further Dialogues of the Buddha*, Vol I, p. 247), with 'unshakeable freedom of mind'. (*The Middle Length Sayings*, Vol. I, p. 253.)

Is *nirvana*, once achieved, permanent, or does it have to be regained? 'Does the Exalted One teach that there is one summit of consciousness, or that there are also several?' 'In my opinion, Potthapada, there is one, and there are also several.' (*Dialogues of the Buddha*, Part I, pp. 251-2.) What about Gotama's *parinibbana*, and did he, in facing death, achieve a final *nirvana*, dialectically conceived? The text reports that Gotama himself sought to convince Ananda that he should not cause remorse in Chunda, whose unintentionally poisonous food was causing his death, by calling attention to the fact. In doing so, he argued: Which of two offerings of food is better, 'The offering of food

which, when a Tathagata has eaten, he attains to supreme
and perfect insight; and the offering of food which, when a
Tathagata has eaten, he passes away by that utter passing
away in which nothing whatever remains behind? These
two offerings of food are of equal fruit. . . .' (*Dialogues of
the Buddha*, Part II, p. 148.) Why? Because one who is
completely willing to accept things as they are is as willing
to die, when it is time for him to die, as he is to achieve
supreme enlightenment, when it is time for him to achieve
supreme enlightenment. It is this complete willingness to
take what comes as it comes which constitutes *nirvana*, not
the dying and utter cessation of desire nor achievement of
ideal fulfilment of desire. The middle way, with its dialectical implications, thus appears to have been expressed by him
at his demise also.

4. Ambiguity or ambivalence, usually abhorred by
Western thinkers, is inherent in the *jhanas*, at least as these
are interpreted here. Gotama's principle aims at complete
ambivalence in that it refers to all things without exception.
As levels of increasing generality of acceptance, *jhanas* are
thus levels of increasing ambiguity or ambivalence. As
levels of dialectically increasing inclusion of opposites,
jhanas are levels of increasing ambiguity. Each *jhana* is
both end and means, but in each higher *jhana* there is more
ambiguity, fusion, or identity, of means and end. *Jhanas*
are, ambiguously, both stages and degrees, steps and not
steps, many and yet one. If all this seems like undue worship
of ambiguity, we may be reminded that Gotama was not a
worshipper, but taught that we should 'neither appreciate
nor depreciate' (*Further Dialogues of the Buddha*, Vol. II,
p. 287), but teach the *dhamma*, i.e., neither appreciate nor
depreciate either ambiguity or definiteness, relativity or
absoluteness, for more than they are worth, but to accept

things with as much ambiguity or as much definiteness as
they have. One who is realistic is willing to accept as much
ambiguity as he is going to get. Each *jhana* is a level of
increasing ambiguity, not only in the sense of increasing
tolerance of each different kind of thing but also in the
sense that the distinction between definiteness and ambiguity itself becomes more ambiguous, unclear, indefinite.
Furthermore, not only are the four emphases noted here
—generality, means-ends, dialectic, and ambiguity—interrelated, but also, as one proceeds up the *jhanas*, distinction
between them becomes increasingly ambiguous. In fact,
one achieves greater ambiguity relative to the ways in which
they are ambiguous. Description of the highest *jhana* as one
in which things are neither definite, nor indefinite, nor both
definite and indefinite, nor neither definite nor indefinite,
appears to be something of a pinnacle of ambiguity.

The eight-fold path, which we have been discussing as
the traditional formulation of the middle way through the
ihanas to *nirvana*, is not necessarily an eight-step path. The
point here stressed is that, regardless of whether or not the
eight are considered as steps, each is a fold in the way, an
area of partial-to-complete realization of *sam*, a variety of
and an ingredient in total *sam-adhi*. Each fold is clearly
labelled with the prefix *samma*. And *sam* means sameness,
ambiguity, universality, equality, regarding willingness to
accept things as they are—in each fold and, finally, in all the
folds together. *Sam* is middle-wayedness between over-
acceptance and under-acceptance, between acceptance of
(attachment to) them as more than they are or less than they
are. Translation of *sam* as 'right view, right resolve', etc.,
or as 'perfect view, perfect resolve', etc. (Cf. *The Middle
Length Sayings*, Vol. I, p. 59), emphasizes the ideal of perfect
or complete acceptance of things as they are, but fails to

convey to most readers the ideal of equanimity which is then
to be perfectly sought. Even though all alternative English
terms which suggest themselves seem both awkward and
inadequate, the use of some alternative seems imperative.

The eight-fold path *is* the middle way, or is middle-
wayed; hence the most obvious, if clumsiest, alternative
appears to be: middle-wayed view, middle-wayed resolve,
middle-wayed speech, middle-wayed action, middle-wayed
livelihood, middle-wayed endeavour, middle-wayed mindfulness and middle-wayed concentration. But the meaning
of 'middle-wayedness' remains unclear without interpretation, and the temptation to substitute inadequate 'moderate'
or 'modest' or 'temperate' for 'middle-wayed' is likely to
prove irresistible. Any term adopted will have to be defined
so that the meaning intended, and not the meaning normally
conveyed by the English term, would be clear. 'Equanimous
view, equanimous resolve', etc., though clumsy, probably
will result in less misunderstanding, partly because there is
considerable ambiguity in the meaning of 'equanimity' in
English. 'Non-attached view, non-attached resolve', etc.,
brings home a basic aspect of what is intended, but leaves
out the middle-wayed character of *sam*. 'Free-in-both-
ways view, free-in-both-ways resolve', etc. (Cf. *Dialogues
of the Buddha*, Part II, p. 70), is suggestive, but clumsy, unclear and inadequate. 'Free view, free resolve', etc., would
require too much explaining of the meaning of 'free' and
succumb too quickly to mistaken interpretations, such as
'irresponsible' (*sam* connotes neither responsibility nor ir-
responsibility, and is not to be found within the responsible-
irresponsible scale, but rather this scale represents merely
one dimension within *sam*). One might use 'realistic view,
realistic resolve', etc., except for the fact that this term is
already too suggestive regarding specific varieties of realism

which are not intended. 'Calming (not just calmed, which is static, but calming which is active) view, calming resolve', etc., is excellent. Even 'relaxing view, relaxing resolve', etc., is a possibility. Any one of these alternatives may be better than 'right view', etc., partly because they leave questions in the minds of readers to investigate further, whereas 'right' or 'perfect' have a kind of finality about them tending to discourage curiosity.

The term chosen might well be different for different occasions, persons, contexts, but for general purposes one is faced with selecting a term which will serve to introduce beginners to what, to be understood, requires one to know already something of the end intended. When *nirvana* is fully comprehended, one somehow experiences all of these —view, resolve, speech, etc.—as together in it in their appropriate proportions. In the end, *samma-samadhi, sam* is not experienced so much as eight distinct types or areas or steps of togetherness, but as all eight ambiguously, because it is complete ambiguity in the sense that it is willingness to accept in all areas. He who analyses the eight as steps has lost his way, or, rather, has not yet found it. When he finds the way, he discovers that he has already arrived at its goal, if not completely, at least genuinely. Steps, as steps, become irrelevant. Seeking to proceed step-wise can only lead away from the already-attained goal. For one who has already achieved a willingness to accept things as they are, seeking more such willingness is like taking a step backwards, or inwards, or like turning a backwards somersault, instead of pursuing something in a forward direction. This need for abandoning step-wise procedure is the same need present in seeking the purpose of one's life; first one looks outside life for its goal; then finds that life is its own goal; and then, further, finds that life lived in such a way that its seeking to find its goal, first outside and then inside, is itself the most ultimate goal—not only 'in this very life' but in this very moment; then any additional search for life's purpose— another step—is not only useless but necessarily misleading, for it can only lead away from, and not toward, a goal already reached.

In *samma-samadhi*, the four truths, the eight folds, the four *jhanas*, the dialectical demands for neither is, nor is not, nor both is and is not, nor neither is nor is not, and all other distinctions are con-fused; not confused but fused together. This does not mean that the distinctions disappear entirely, but rather that interest in one distinction as more important than another, if this means more important than it is, becomes detached and replaced by a willingness to seek each distinction for what it is. A distinction does not stand alone by itself; neither is it so all-important that it should subordinate all life to it; rather it finds itself in the context of life, and is to be regarded with equanimity, as neither more isolated nor less isolated than it is, neither more important nor less important than it is, neither more real nor less real than it is. *Nirvana* is a state in which things, folds, dimensions are intended neither as distinct nor indistinct or neither as more distinct nor more indistinct than they are, but are held in equanimous regard. It is the willingness with which they are regarded that is completely or perfectly ambiguous, general, universal. It is this willingness which frees one from anguish. *Samma-sambodhi* is final realization of *nirvana*; and *sam-bodhi* and *bodhi-sattva*, wisdom about existence and the existence of wisdom, or achievement of *nirvana* and embodiment of *nirvana* in and as existence itself, are also the same, or *sam*, or *samadhi*, or *samma-samadhi*.

What, then, is *nirvana*? It is not something either in a next life or beyond life, but something in this very life, in

this very moment. It is not something just at the end of the
eight-fold path, a step beyond the last step, but something
which may be present in all folds, in every aspect of life. It
is not something apart from life, for specialists like monks,
recluses, or sanyassins, yet also it usually is not obtained
without effort, attention, practice, and sufficiently favourable conditions. It is not something which is a goal separated
from the means, but something in which means and end
are fused in such a way that it is the end which predominates.
It is not a trance-like ecstasy, but an attitude of willingness
to appreciate whatever is. *Nirvana* is *moksha* or *mukti*,
release from tension, freedom from anxiety, relaxed living.
'Formerly I, monks, as well as now, lay down simply
anguish and the stopping of anguish.' (*The Middle Length
Sayings*, Vol. I, p. 180.) 'Putting away flurry and worry, he
remains free from fretfulness, and with heart serene within,
he purifies himself of irritability and vexation of spirit.
Putting away wavering, he remains as one passed beyond
perplexity; and no longer in suspense as to what is good, he
purifies his mind of doubt.' (*Dialogues of the Buddha*, Part
I, p. 82.) Having achieved *nirvana* 'is like a deer living in a
forest who might lie down on a heap of snares but is not
caught by it. . . . It is like a deer . . . roaming the forest
slopes, who walks confidently, stands confidently, sits down
confidently, goes to sleep confidently.' (*The Middle Length
Sayings*, Vol. I, p. 218.)

GREED FOR VIEWS

'MARVELLOUS it is, sir, the great gifts and powers of the Samana Gotama in withholding his own theories and inviting the discussion of those of others.' (*Dialogues of the Buddha*, Part III, p. 37.) Gotama's simple yet subtle doctrine, though repeated again and again, remained largely incredible to many of his hearers, as it did also to later followers. He was asked repeatedly whether his *dhamma* applied to this or that specific problem and how it compared with this or that specific view. In seeking to give assurance that it applied universally, he, or scholars after him, systematically reviewed all the known theories on various topics, repudiating each in turn and condemning all whose devotion to any view appeared as a manifestation of avidity, passion, anxiety or greed. Long lists of theories of those 'who reconstruct the past and arrange the future, or who do both, whose speculations are concerned with both . . . in sixty-two ways . . .' (*Dialogues of the Buddha*, Part I, p. 52) are summarized as follows at the end of the Brahmagala Sutta which is devoted to them:

'Of these, brethren, those recluses and brahmans who are Eternalists, who in four ways maintain that the soul and the world are eternal; (2) those who are Semi-eternalists, who in four ways maintain that the soul and the world are partly eternal and partly not; (3) those who are Extensionists, who in four ways maintain the infinity of the finiteness of the world; (4) those who are Eel-wrigglers, who when a question is put to them on this or that resort, in four ways, to equivocation, to wriggling like eels;[7] (5) those who are Fortuitous-originists, who in two ways maintain that the soul and the world arose without a cause; (6) those who in any of these eighteen ways reconstruct the past; (7) those who hold the doctrine of a conscious existence after death, who maintain in sixteen ways[8] that the soul after death is conscious; (8) those who hold the doctrine of an unconscious existence after death, who maintain in eight ways

---

[7] Those who resort to eel-wriggling say: 'I don't take it thus. I don't take it the other way. But I advance no different opinion. And I don't deny your position. And I don't say it is neither the one, nor the other.' (*Dialogues of the Buddha*, Part I, p. 38.) This eel-wriggling position, which might easily be mistaken for Gotama's, represents the plight of one who fears to take a stand lest he be embarrassed by it. Such embarrassment signifies undue attachment to reputation. If reputation, like other things, is transient, attachment to it, and consequent embarrassment, is needless. Gotama felt no need for attachment to a position requiring equivocation. The discourse on the fourth variety of eel-wriggling is devoted to citing four examples of the 'principle of four-cornered negation', each 'corner' of which the eel-wriggler equivocates about: 'And it is by reason of his dullness, his stupidity, that when a question on this or that is put to him, he resorts to equivocation . . . "If you ask me whether there is another world—well, if I thought there were, I would say so. But I don't say so. And I don't think it is thus or thus. And I don't think it is otherwise. And I don't deny it. And I don't say there neither is, nor is not, another world." Thus does he advocate, and in like manner about each of such propositions as the following: (A) (2) There is not another world. (3) There both is, and is not, another world. (4) There neither is, nor is not, another world. (B)(1) There are chance beings (so called because they spring into existence, either here or in another world without the intervention of parents, and seem therefore to come without a cause). (2) There are no such beings. (3) There both are, and are not, such beings. (4) There neither are, nor are not, such beings. (C) (1) There is fruit, result, of good and bad actions. (2) There is not. (3) There both is, and is not. (4) There neither is, nor is not. (D) (1) A man who has penetrated to the truth continues to exist after death. (2) He does not. (3) He both does, and does not. (4) He neither does, nor does not.' (*Dialogues of the Buddha*, Part I, pp. 39–40.)

[8] 'They say of the soul: "The soul after death, not subject to decay, and conscious, (1) has form, (2) is formless, (3) has, and has not, form, (4) neither has, nor has not, form, (5) is finite, (6) is infinite, (7) is both, (8) is neither, (9) has one mode of consciousness, (10) has various modes of consciousness, (11) has limited consciousness, (12) has infinite consciousness, (13) is altogether happy, (14) is altogether miserable, (15) is both, (16) is neither." ' (*Ibid.*, p. 44.)

that the soul after death is unconscious; (9) those who maintain in eight ways that the soul after death is neither conscious nor unconscious; (10) those who are Annihilationists, who maintain in seven ways the cutting off, the destruction, the annihilation of a living being; (11) those who hold the doctrine of happiness in this life, who in five ways maintain the complete salvation in this visible world, of a living being. That opinion of theirs is based on the personal sensations, on the worry and writhing consequent thereon, of those . . . who . . . are subject to all kinds of craving. . . . For whosoever . . . are thus reconstructors of the past or arrangers of the future, or who are both, . . . all of them are entrapped in the net of these sixty-two modes; this way and that way they may flounder, but they are included in it, caught in it. Just as when a skilful fisherman . . . should drag a tiny pool of water with a fine-meshed net he might fairly think: "Whatever fish of size in this pond, every one will be in this net; flounder about as they may, they will be included in it, and caught"—just so it is that these speculators about the past and the future, in this net, flounder as they may, they are included and caught.' (*Dialogues of the Buddha*, Part I, pp. 52–4.)

A shorter list of ten questions which Gotama refused to settle appears several times in the suttas: 'Is the world eternal?' 'That, Potthapada, is a matter on which I have expressed no opinion.' (*Dialogues of the Buddha*, Part I, p. 254.) Is the world not eternal? Is the world finite? Is the world infinite? Is the soul the same as the body? Is the soul one thing, and the body another? Does one who has gained the truth live again after death? Does he not live again after death? Does he both live again, and not live again, after death? Does he neither live again, nor not live again, after death? To each he replied: 'That too, Pottha-

pada, is a matter on which I have expressed no opinion.'
'But why . . .?' 'This question is not calculated to profit, is
not concerned with the *dhamma*, it does not redound even
to the elements of right conduct, nor to detachment, nor to
purification from lusts, nor to quietude, nor to tranquillization of heart, nor to real knowledge, nor to the insight (of
the higher stages of the Path), nor to *Nirvana*. Therefore is
it that I express no opinion upon it.' 'Then what is it that
the Exalted One *has* determined?' 'I have expounded what
pain (*dukkha*) is; . . . the origin of pain; . . . cessation of
pain; . . . what is the method by which one may reach the
cessation of pain.' 'And why . . .?' 'Because that . . . is
calculated to profit. . . .' (*Ibid.*, pp. 254–5.)

After another dialogue in which Gotama gives non-
committal answers to the foregoing ten questions, Vaccha
asks: 'To each and all of my questions, Gotama, you have
answered in the negative. What, pray, is the danger you discern in these views which makes you scout them all?' 'To
hold that the world is eternal—or to hold that it is not, or
to agree to any other of the propositions you adduce,
Vaccha—is the thicket of theorizing, the wilderness of
theorizing, the tangle of theorizing, the bondage and the
shackles of theorizing, attended by ill, distress, perturba-
tion and fever; it conduces not to aversion, passionlessness,
tranquillity, peace, illumination and *Nirvana*.' 'Is there any
view which you have adopted, Gotama?' 'The adoption of
views is a term discarded for the truth-finder, who has had
actual vision of the nature, origin and cessation of things
material—of feelings—of perception—of plastic forces—
and of consciousness. Therefore it is that, by destroying,
stilling, suppressing, discarding and renouncing all suppos-
ings, all imaginings, and all tendencies to the pride of saying I or mine, the truth-finder is delivered because no fuel

is left to keep such things going.' 'When his heart is thus delivered, Gotama, where is an almsman reborn hereafter?' 'Reborn does not apply to him.' 'Then he is not reborn?' 'Not-reborn does not apply.' 'Then he is both reborn and not reborn?' 'Reborn and not-reborn does not apply.' 'Then he is neither reborn nor not reborn?' 'Neither reborn nor not-reborn does not apply to him.' 'To each and all of my questions, Gotama, you have replied in the negative. I am at a loss and bewildered; the measure of confidence you inspired by our former talk has disappeared.' 'You ought to be at a loss and bewildered, Vaccha. For this doctrine is profound, recondite, hard to comprehend, excellent, beyond dialectic, subtle, only to be understood by the wise. To you it is difficult—who hold other views and belong to another faith and objective, with a different allegiance and a different master. So I in turn will question you, for such answer as you see fit to give. What think you, Vaccha?—If there were a blaze in front of you, would you know it?' 'Yes.' 'If you were asked what made that fire blaze, could you give an answer?' 'I should answer that what made it blaze, was the fuel. . . .' 'If the fire went out, would you know it had gone out?' 'Yes.' 'If now you were asked in what direction the fire had gone, whether to east, west, north or south, could you give an answer?' 'The answer does not apply.' (*Further Dialogues of the Buddha,* Vol. I, pp. 342–4. *See also The Middle Length Sayings,* Vol. II, pp. 162–7.)

'There are some samanas and brahmans, Potthapada, who hold the following opinion, indulge in the following speculation: "The soul is perfectly happy and healthy after death." And I went to them, and asked them whether that was their view or not. And they acknowledged that it was. And I asked them whether, so far as they were in the habit of knowing or perceiving it, the world (that is, the people in the world) was perfectly happy, and they answered: "No." Then I asked them: "Or further, Sirs, can you maintain that yourselves for a whole night, or for a whole day, or even for half a night or day, you have ever been perfectly happy?" And they answered: "No." Then I said to them: "Or further, Sirs, do you know a way, or a method, by which you can realize a state that is altogether happy?" And still to that question they answered: "No." And then I said: "Or have you, Sirs, ever heard the voices of gods who had realized rebirth in a perfectly happy world', saying: 'Be earnest, O men, and direct in effort, towards the realization of a world of perfect happiness. For we, in consequence of similar effort, have been reborn in such a world'?" And still they answered: "No." Now what think you as to that, Potthapada? That being so, does not the talk of those samanas and brahmans turn out to be without good ground? ... Then just so also, Potthapada, with the samanas and brahmans who talk about the soul being perfectly happy and healthy after death.' (*Dialogues of the Buddha*, Part I, pp. 257–9.)

'On two things, Kaccana, does this world generally base its view—on existence and on non-existence. Now he who with right insight sees the arising of the world as it really is, does not believe in the non-existence of the world. But, Kaccana, he who with right insight sees the ceasing of the world as it really is, does not believe in the existence of the world. Grasping after systems, imprisoned by dogmas is the world, Kaccana, for the most part. And he who does not go after, does not grasp at, does not take his stand on this system-grasping, this dogma, this mental bias—such an one does not say "it is my soul". He who thinks, "that which arises is but ill; that which ceases, it is ill", such an one has no doubts, no perplexity. In this matter, knowledge not borrowed from others comes to him. Thus far, Kaccana, goes right view. "All exists," Kaccana—that is one extreme. "Nought exists," Kaccana—that is the other extreme. Not approaching either extreme, Kaccana, the Tathagata teaches you a doctrine by the middle way.' (*The Book of the Kindred Sayings*, Vol. III, p. 114.)

'Whether the beginning of things be revealed, or whether it be not, the object for which I teach the *dhamma* is this: that it leads to the thorough destruction of ill for the doer thereof. . . . If then, Sunakkhatta, it matters not to that object whether the beginning of things be revealed, or whether it is not, of what use to you would it be to have the beginning of things revealed?' (*Dialogues of the Buddha*, Part III, pp. 9, 10.)

'Monks, there are these three grounds of sectarian tenets, which, though strictly questioned, investigated and discussed by wise men, persist in a traditional doctrine of inaction. What three? There are certain recluses and brahmins who teach thus, who hold this view: Whatsoever weal or woe or neutral feeling is experienced, all that is due to some previous action. There are others who teach: Whatsoever weal or woe or neutral feeling is experienced, all that is due to the creation of a supreme deity. Others teach that all such are uncaused and unconditioned. . . . Now, monks, as to those recluses and brahmins who hold and teach the first of these views, I approach them and say: "Is it true, as they say, that you worthy sirs teach that . . . all is due to former action?" Thus questioned by me they reply: "Yes, we do." Then I say to them: "So then, owing to a previous action, men will become murderers, thieves, unchaste, liars, slanderers, abusive, babblers, covetous, malicious, and perverse in view. Thus for those who fall back on the former deed as the essential reason there is neither desire to do, nor effort to do, nor necessity to do this deed or abstain from that deed. So then, the necessity for action or inaction not being found to exist in truth and verity, the term 'recluse' cannot be reasonably applied to yourselves, since you live in a state of bewilderment with faculties unrewarded." Such, monks, is my first reasonable rebuke to those recluses and brahmins who teach thus, who hold such views. Again, monks, as to those recluses and brahmins who hold and teach the second of these views, I approach them and say: "Is it true, as they say, that you worthy sirs teach that . . . all this is due to the creation of a supreme deity?" Thus questioned by me they reply: "Yes, we do." Then I say to them: "So then, owing to the creation of a supreme deity, men will become murderers . . . and perverse in view. Thus for those who fall back on the creation of a supreme deity as the essential reason, there is neither desire to do, nor effort to do, nor necessity to do this deed or abstain from that deed. So then, the necessity for action or inaction not being found to exist in truth and verity, the term 'recluse' cannot reasonably be applied to yourselves, since you live in a state of bewilderment with faculties unrewarded." Such, monks, is my second reasonable rebuke to those recluses and brahmins who thus teach, who hold such views. Again, monks, as to those recluses and brahmins who teach thus, who hold this view: Whatsoever weal or woe or neutral feeling is experienced, all that is uncaused and unconditioned—I approach them and say: "Is it true, as they say, that you worthy sirs teach that . . . all this is uncaused and unconditioned?" Thus questioned by me they reply: "Yes, we do." Then I say to them: "So then, owing to no cause or condition at all, men will become murderers, thieves . . . and perverse in view. Thus for those who fall back on the uncaused and unconditioned as the essential, there is neither desire to do, nor effort to do, nor necessity to do this deed or to abstain from that deed. So, then, the necessity for action or inaction not being found to exist in truth and verity, the term 'recluse' cannot be reasonably applied to yourselves. . . ." Such, monks, is my third reasonable rebuke to those recluses and brahmins who hold and teach these views. And these are the three grounds of sectarian tenets which, though strictly questioned, investigated and discussed by wise men, persist in a traditional doctrine of inaction.' (*The Book of the Gradual Sayings*, Vol. I, pp. 157–9.)

Malunkya-putta, reflecting upon the views which Gotama had 'left unexpounded, omitted and dismissed without answer—such as: The world is eternal', etc., complained: 'I do not like his not expounding these things to me; I resent it; I will go to him and question him hereon. If he definitely either accepts or rejects any of these propositions, I will follow the higher life under the Lord; but if he fails to expound them, I will throw up my training as an almsman and will revert to the lower plane of a layman.' When he demanded of Gotama a straight answer—If you know, tell me, and if you don't know, say you don't know—Gotama replied: 'Did I ever promise you, Malunkya-putta, that, if you followed the higher life under me, I would tell you whether the world is eternal, and all the rest of it?' 'No, sir.' . . . 'It comes to this then that I have never promised, nor did you stipulate that, as a condition of your following the higher life under me, I should expound these matters to you. This being so, who are you . . . to reject them? If, Malunkya-putta, a man were to say he would not follow the higher life under the Lord until the Lord had answered all the questions you enumerate, he would get no answer from the Truth-finder before death overtook him. It is just as if a man were transfixed by an arrow heavily coated with poison, and his friends and kinsfolk were to get him a leech expert in dealing with arrow-wounds, but the man were to declare he would not have the arrow taken out until he knew whether the archer who had shot him was a noble or a brahmin or a middle-class man or a peasant, what the archer's name and lineage was, whether he was tall or short or of medium height, whether he was black or dark or fair. . . . The man would never get to know all this before death overtook him. And just in the same way, if a man were to say that he would not follow the higher life under the Lord until the Lord had answered this pack of questions, he would get no answer from the Truth-finder before death overtook him. The higher life is not contingent on the truth of any thesis that the world either is or is not eternal. In either case, as in each of the other theses you adduce, there still abides the fact of birth, decay and death; there still abide the facts of grief and tribulation, of ill, sorrow and distraction—of all of which I proclaim the extirpation here and now.' (*Further Dialogues of the Buddha*, Vol. I, pp. 305–6. *See also The Middle Length Sayings*, Vol. II, pp. 97–101.)

Once Gotama was asked: 'What is the cause, the reason, why to the learned Ariyan listener doubt arises not as to the unexplained points?' 'Verily, it is by view-stopping, monk, that doubt arises not . . . as to unexplained points. "Is the tathagata after death?"—this is but a view-issue. . . . The unlearned average man understands not view, understands not view-origin, understands not view-stopping, understands not the stepping of the way to view-stopping. For him view grows. . . . But the learned Ariyan listener understands view, its origin, its stopping. . . . For him view is stopped. . . . Thus knowing . . . (he) is thus subject to the inexplicable as to unexplained points. Thus knowing . . . (he) is not afraid, trembles not, wavers not, shakes not, nor falls to quaking concerning these points. "Is the tathagata after death?" and the like. . . . These, monks, are but issues of craving . . . , are but a source of remorse.' (*The Book of the Gradual Sayings*, Vol. IV, pp. 39–40.)

A story appearing in the suttas, though apparently not originating with Gotama, argues the futility of seeking answers to metaphysical questions. Whether intended as humorous, cynical or serious, the reader will have to decide for himself. When one seeker wondered where do the four great elements, earth, water, fire, and wind, go when they finally disappear, he sought the answer first from the great kings, then the great gods, then the king of the gods, etc., until he came finally to Brahma himself. The Great Brahma 'took that brother by the arm and led him aside and said: "The gods . . . hold me to be such that there is nothing I cannot see, nothing I have not understood, nothing I have not realized. Therefore I have no answer in their presence. I do not know, brother, where those four great elements . . . cease. . . . Therefore you have done wrong, have acted ill, in that, ignoring the Exalted One, you have undertaken this long search. . . ."' (*Dialogues of the Buddha*, Part I, p. 282.)

Did the Gotama's refusal to express an opinion regarding metaphysical questions imply that they could have no solution? No. 'It is just like a man blind from birth who could not see black or white, blue or yellow, or red or pink things, who could not see level or rough ground, the stars, or the sun and moon, and who should affirm that there are no such things, and that no one could see them—on the ground forsooth that, as he himself had no knowledge or vision of them, therefore they were non-existent. In so saying would he say aright?' 'No, Gotama.' 'These things do exist and there are those who can see them; and consequently he would be wrong in saying they were non-existent merely because he could not see them.' (*Further Dialogues of the Buddha*, Vol. II, p. 115.) But also, I 'do not say that all that one has seen should be spoken of. Yet I do not say that all that one has seen should not be spoken of.' (*The Book of the Gradual Sayings*, Vol. II, pp. 179–80. Tr. F. L. Woodward, Luzac and Co., Ltd., London, 1933, 1952.) He merely objected, in the words of Sariputta, to making 'difficulty where there is none'. (*Ibid.*, p. 168.)[9]

[9] Gotama was quizzed not only regarding theories, but regarding seemingly endless numbers of activities which aroused interest. Regarding all of them, he had developed a reputation for holding aloof. Examples: ballad recitations, acrobatic feats, combats by elephants, bulls, cocks, games on boards with eight, or with ten, rows of squares, throwing dice, guessing games, games with balls, turning somersaults, embroideries, bracelets, conversation about women, heroes, ghosts, foods, gossip, palmistry, sacrificing to the gods, lucky charms and times and places, predicting weather and crops, counting, magic, worship, applying collyrium to the eyes, etc. (Cf. *Dialogues of the Buddha*, Part I, pp. 3–26.)

10

SOUL OR NO SOUL?

ALTHOUGH Gotama's view regarding soul should be clear from the foregoing, the importance of the no-soul doctrine in the history of Buddhism warrants further reference to statements bearing explicitly on the subject. The existence of an enduring soul is explicitly and repeatedly denied in the Putakas. For example: 'This, monks, is called going to wrong views . . .: "Whatever is this self for me that speaks, that experiences and knows, that experiences now here, now there, the fruition of deeds that are lovely and that are depraved, it is this self for me that is permanent, stable, eternal, not subject to change, that will stand firm like unto the eternal." ' (*The Middle Length Sayings*, Vol. I, p. 11.) On the other hand, when 'a certain brahman . . . said to the Exalted One: "This, Master Gotama, is my avowal, this is my view: There is no self-agency, no other agency," Gotama replied, "Never, brahman, have I seen or heard of such an avowal, such a view. Pray, how can one step onwards, how can one step back, yet say: There is no self-agency; there is no other agency? What think you, brahman, is there such a thing as initiation?" "Yes, sir." . . . "Well, brahman, since there is initiative and men are known to initiate, this is among men the self-agency, this is the other agency." ' (*The Book of the Gradual Sayings*, Vol. III, pp. 237–8.)

But neither of the two foregoing quotations expresses

what is most typical of Gotama's view: 'In so many ways, Ananda, there is a refraining from declarations concerning the soul.' (*Dialogues of the Buddha*, Part II, p. 63.) Gotama's refusal to take sides in this issue is perhaps best expressed in an incident where Vacchagotta, the wanderer, sought a clear-cut answer: ' "Now, good Gotama, is there a self?" When he had spoken thus, the lord became silent. "What, then, good Gotama, is there not a self?" And a second time the lord became silent. Then the wanderer, Vacchagotta, rising from his seat, departed. Then, soon after his departure, the venerable Ananda spoke thus to the lord: "Why, lord, did not the lord answer Vacchagotta the wanderer's question?" "If I . . . should have answered that there is a self, this, Ananda, would have been a siding-in with those recluses and brahmans who are Eternalists. If I . . . should have answered that there is not a self, this, Ananda, would have been a siding-in with those recluses and brahmans who are Annihilationists." ' (*The Book of the Kindred Sayings*, Vol. IV, quoted in A. K. Coomaraswamy and I. B. Horner, *The Living Thoughts of Gotama The Buddha*, p. 149. Cassell and Co., Ltd., London, 1948.)

He persistently avoided taking sides in this issue because it was so insignificant compared with the main issue: anguish and the stopping of anguish. To be concerned with the issue, soul versus non-soul, is to be in bondage to 'craving for becoming and non-becoming'. (*The Middle Length Sayings*, Vol. I, p. 142.) But 'when a brother, Ananda, does not regard soul under these aspects—either as feeling, or as non-sentient, or as having feeling–then he, thus refraining from such views, grasps at nothing whatever in the world; and not grasping he trembles not; and trembling not, he by himself attains to perfect peace'. (*Dialogues of the Buddha*, Part II, p. 65.) One who willingly accepts things as they are is equally willing to accept soul or no soul, whichever happens to exist. Taking sides in a useless controversy, hence expressing unwillingness to accept things as they are if the other side happens to be true, is a folly in which Gotama refused to indulge.

To each of a whole series of suggested views concerning the nature of self, summarized as follows, attention is called to the fact that such a view is 'an activity', a concern, an attachment, an anxiety: Some 'regard the body as the self. This regarding is an activity. . . . Maybe he regards not the body as the self, yet he regards the self as possessing body; and this view also is an activity. . . . Maybe he regards not body as self, regards not the self as possessing a body, yet he regards body as being in the self. And this view also is an activity. . . . Maybe he regards not body as the self, regards not the self as possessing body, regards not body as being in the self—yet he regards the self as being in the body. And this view is an activity. . . . Maybe he . . . regards feeling as the self . . . regards perception, the activities, regards consciousness as the self. . . . Maybe, however, brethren, he (holds none of these views, but yet) has this belief: "That is the self; that is the world; that hereafter shall I become permanent, lasting, eternal, not subject to change. . . ." But this eternalist belief also, brethren, is an activity. . . . Maybe he regards not body as the self, regards not feeling, perception, the activities, consciousness as the self . . . regards not the self as being in consciousness. . . . Maybe he has not this view: "That is the self, that is the world, that hereafter I shall become permanent, lasting, eternal, not subject to change. . . ." Yet in spite of this, maybe he is doubting, wavering, not firmly established in the true (way). But this very doubting, this wavering, this being not established in the true (way)—this is an activity.' (*The Book of the*

Kindred Sayings, Vol. III, pp. 82–4.) Gotama's typical response, 'Nevertheless I do not say either the one or the other' (*Dialogues of the Buddha*, Part I, p. 204), was aimed at rest from such activity or at cessation of anxiety.

Persistent attempts at analysis of the nature of experience by others, even in the spirit of Gotama, to point out in detail the kinds of 'craving that ensnares', beget the same answer. For example: 'There are eighteen thoughts which are haunted by craving concerning the inner self and eighteen which are haunted by craving concerning what is external to self. Now of what sorts are the former? When there is the thought: I am, there come the thoughts: I am in this world: I am thus: I am otherwise: I am not eternal: I am eternal: Should I be: Should I be in this world: Should I be thus: Should I be otherwise: May I become: May I become in this world: May I become thus: May I become otherwise: Shall I become: Shall I become in this world: Shall I become thus: Shall I become otherwise.' (*The Book of the Gradual Sayings*, Vol. II, p. 226.) These eighteen, plus eighteen concerning the external self, make thirty-six, and when compounded by past, present, and future, constitute one hundred and eight types of craving. But 'Then thought I: Meticulous analysis of the phenomena has arisen within me and consequently concentration has passed away . . .; I will take measures to stop this meticulosity of analysis too from occurring in the future.' (*Further Dialogues of the Buddha*, Vol. II, p. 247.) Again, when a certain brother inquired of the Exalted One: 'Are these five grasping-groups, lord, to wit: the grasping body-group, the grasping feeling-group, the grasping perception-group, the grasping activities and the grasping consciousness-groups?' and 'Now this same grasping, lord—is it those five grasping-groups, or is grasping something apart from those five groups?' he replied: 'No indeed, brother, this same grasping is not those five grasping-groups, nor yet is it something apart from those five groups. But where there is desire and lust, there also is grasping.' (*The Book of the Kindred Sayings*, Vol. III, p. 85.)

What about *karma*? This conception, so fundamental to Gotama's cultural heritage, was a part of the very language in which he and his disciples thought and spoke. That the conception has lived on and played an important role in later Buddhist explanations, no one will wish to deny. But that Gotama was committed to the concept of *karma* as essential to his own doctrine must be rejected. His principle, to stop frustration stop desiring what will not be attained, holds regardless of whether or not there is a law of *karma*. If there is a law of *karma*, then accept it; if there is none, accept this likewise. When Siha asked Gotama: 'I have heard that the Samana Gotama has no belief in *karma*; he teaches a law of non-*karma*. . . . Now do those . . . speak rightly?' he replied, 'In a way, Siha, one speaking rightly might say of me "The Samana Gotama has no belief in *karma*; he teaches a law of non-*karma*. . . ." Again, in a way, one speaking rightly might say of me "The Samana Gotama has belief in *karma*; that he teaches a law of *karma*. . . .' (*Vinaya Texts*, Part II, p. 110. Tr. T. W. Rhys Davids and Herman Oldenberg, Oxford U. Press, London, 1882.)

Gotama is reported to have argued against the Jain view of gaining merit and removing demerit by austerities. The Jain view, as reported, is that if there is 'an evil deed that was formerly done by you, wear it away by this severe austerity. . . . Thus by burning up, making an end of former deeds, by the non-doing of new deeds, there is no flowing in the future. . . .' Gotama's supposedly devastating rebuttal of the Jain view is recorded thus: 'But do you know that you yourselves were in the past, that you were not not?' 'Not this, your reverence.' 'But do you know that you yourselves did this evil deed in the past, that you did not not do it?' 'Not this, your reverence.' 'But do you know you did not do an evil deed like this or like that?' 'Not this, your reverence.' 'But do you know that so much ill is worn away, or that so much ill is to be worn away, or that when so much ill is worn away, all ill will become worn away?' 'Not this, your reverence.' 'From what you say you do not know then whether you yourselves were in the past, whether you were not not; you do not know whether in the past you yourselves did this evil deed, whether you did not not do it; you do not know whether you did an evil deed like this or like that; you do not know so much ill is worn away, or that so much ill is to be worn away, or that when such much ill is worn away all ill will become worn away. . . .' (*Middle Length Sayings*, Vol. I, pp. 122–3.) 'I assert that noble birth does not make a good man.' (*Further Dialogues of the Buddha*, Vol. II, p. 101.) Since one cannot rely on his knowledge, or ignorance, of the way the law of *karma* works, if he is to achieve salvation with assurance, it must be by some other means. Evil consists in anxiety, which is caused by craving. Now regardless of whether one's present craving is caused by past *karma* or not caused by past *karma*, one still has the task of stopping craving, and this task requires present effort. Why not concentrate upon what is necessary and ignore matters which are irrelevant? In fact, interest in *karma* involves interest in future rewards, hence in rebirth, attachment to a persisting soul, a demand for justice, and taking sides regarding explanations. To the extent that one is attached to *karma*, he deviates from the middle way.

Did Gotama believe in rebirth? 'All beings, sire, are mortal; they finish with death.' (*The Book of the Kindred*

Sayings, Vol. I, p. 122. Tr. C. A. F. Rhys Davids, Luzac and Co., Ltd., London, 1917, 1950.) This view, attributed to the Exalted One, is opposed to the numerous statements presupposing rebirth. Gotama's principle implies willingness to accept rebirth or no rebirth, whichever is to come. When a brahman accused him, 'Master Gotama is against rebirth,' he replied in the affirmative, 'but not in the way you mean.' (*The Book of the Gradual Sayings*, Vol. IV, p. 120.) 'A new doctrine, Cunda, do I teach for subduing the mental intoxicants that are generated even in this present life. I teach not a doctrine for the extirpation of intoxicants in the future life only, but one for the subduing them now, and also for extirpating them in the after life.' (*Dialogues of the Buddha*, Part III, p. 121.) His doctrine is intended as universal and for all times, now and in the future. But it is not directed toward the future. 'I have shown my disciples the way whereby, by the eradication of cankers, they—here and now, of and by themselves—know, realize, enter on, and abide in that deliverance of heart and mind in which cankers are no more.' (*Further Dialogues of the Buddha*, Vol. II, p. 12.)

The solution to the problem of stopping anguish does not depend upon settling the question of whether or not there is rebirth, i.e., rebirth in another body. 'It is in this fathom-long carcass, friend, with its impressions and its ideas, that, I declare, lies the world, and the cause of the world, and the cessation of the world, and the course of action that leads to the cessation of the world.' (*The Book of the Kindred Sayings*, Vol. I, p. 86. *See also The Book of the Gradual Sayings*, Vol. II, p. 57.) 'Were there no grasping of any sort or kind whatever by anyone at anything—that is to say, no grasping at the things of sense, no grasping through speculative opinions, no grasping after mere rule and ritual, no grasping through theories of soul—then there being no grasping whatever, would there, owing to this cessation of grasping, be any appearance of becoming?' 'There would not, lord.' (*Dialogues of the Buddha*, Part II, pp. 53–4.) When the four 'truths are grasped and known the craving for future life is rooted out, that which leads to renewed becoming is destroyed, and then there is no more birth'. (*Ibid.*, p. 96.) 'What is the cord of rebirth?' 'That desire, that lust, that lure, that craving, those graspings after systems, that mental standpoint, that dogmatic bias which is concerned with body—that is called "the cord of rebirth". The ceasing of these is called "the ceasing of the cord of rebirth".' (*The Book of the Kindred Sayings*, Vol. III, p. 157.)

'Some recluses and brahmans there are who hold and affirm that there is no such thing as the stilling of continuing existence, while others again assert the contrary. What think you, sirs? Are not these two schools diametrically opposed one to the other?' 'Yes, sir.' 'In this case a man of intelligence says to himself that he personally has neither seen what those affirm who deny that existence can be stilled, nor discovered what those others affirm who assert that it can; nor does he feel it proper, without knowing or seeing for himself, definitely to commit himself to one side or the other as representing the absolute truth where all else is error.' (*Further Dialogues of the Buddha*, Vol. I, p. 295.) It is not stilling of existence, but stilling of craving, which is the goal. Gotama sought suppression of rebirth of craving. The term 'rebirth' ambiguously denotes rebirth of craving, rebirth of desire, rebirth of consciousness, either in a next moment, next hour, next day, etc., and either in this same body only or in another body or bodies only or both in this and in another body or bodies. Gotama was definitely against rebirth of craving, but he was neither for nor against the other types of rebirth. The middle way involves a willingness to accept either rebirth or no rebirth of consciousness in another life. But the problem of rebirth of craving is the most universal, as well as the most significant and most urgent, for it pertains to all times, regardless of whether it be this moment, this life, or future lives if there are to be future lives. If one has solved this problem and is freed from craving, then all other problems cease to be problems, for with respect to them he has ceased to crave. 'Of such a brother, Ananda, whose heart is thus set free, if any one should say: "His creed is that an Arahant goes on after death," that were absurd. Or: "His creed is that an Arahant does not go on . . . does, and yet does not, go on . . . neither goes on nor goes not on after death," all that were absurd.' (*Dialogues of the Buddha*, Part II, p. 65.) They are absurd because they do not conduce to 'happy living in this very life'. (*The Book of the Gradual Sayings*, Vol. II, p. 52.)

Apparently Gotama did not object to talking about rebirths, previous births, and even the probable status of departed disciples, but he did so only as instrumental to clarifying his main points in the intellectual idiom of his day. 'My end in view is not to cajole or delude folk, nor is it to get for myself gains of repute or fame or profit, nor is it to advertise myself as revealing the prospective states hereafter of my disciples dead and gone. No; it is because there are young men who believe and are filled with enthusiasm and with gladness, who, on hearing this revelation, concentrate their whole hearts on imitating it all—to their own abiding good and welfare.' (*Further Dialogues of the Buddha*, Vol. I, p. 331.)

11

SANGHA

THE Pali term, *sangha*, like its Sanskrit ancestor, *sam-gha*, means, generally, any close contact or any number of people living together for a certain purpose. Like the English words, society and association, its meaning ranges all the way from a loose but continuing fellowship of two or more persons to any complex, highly organized and regulated, permanently established institution. What later hardened into an 'Order' of yellow-robed monks requiring two hundred and twenty-seven rules of observance and fortnightly confessions of infractions had its origins in a way of life preceding Gotama's time. 'It is well known that the history of religious mendicancy in India may be traced to remote antiquity. The religious mendicants formed a widespread, populous, and influential community in Northern India even in the sixth century, B.C. They lived outside social and communal organizations, but they constituted by themselves a well-defined community. They had internal relations amongst themselves—communal customs, recognized manners and usages, and distinctive ideas and practices. There were also numerous sectarian parties among them called Sanghas or Ganas, and one of them, which afterwards became the most influential in history, was led by the world-famous Prince of the Sakya clan. Now this Sangha which recognized Buddha as their leader partook no doubt of the general characteristics of all Paribbajakas (religious mendicants) and followed generally their common customs and usages. Many features of Buddhist monachism, therefore, point back to earlier times than the foundation of the Buddhist Sangha itself.' (Sukumar Dutt, *Early Buddhist Monachism*, p. 16. Kegan Paul, Trench, Trubner and Co., Ltd., London, 1924.) 'All this indicates that there must have been a fairly long development of the discipline of the community prior to the final completion of the Vinayapitaka, and that the bulk of the rules originated, not all at once, but gradually. On the other hand it has been shown that many of the regulations of the order of the community are identical with those which were in vogue among other sects of ascetics before Buddha.' (Maurice Winternitz, *A History of Indian Literature*, Vol. II, p. 26. University of Calcutta, 1933.)

Evidence that Gotama himself had no intention of imposing a specific set of regulations upon his followers may be seen in the following report. When Gotama was getting old, ill, and about to die, Ananda expressed the hope that Gotama 'would not pass away until at least he had left instructions as touching the Order'. 'What, then, Ananda? Does the Order expect that of me? I have preached the truth without making any distinction between exoteric and esoteric doctrine; for in respect of the truths, Ananda, the Tathagata has no such thing as the closed fist of a teacher, who keeps some things back. Surely, Ananda, should there be any one who harbours the thought, "It is I who will lead the brotherhood", or, "The Order is dependent upon me", it is he who should lay down instructions in any matter concerning the Order. Now the Tathagata, Ananda, thinks not that it is he who should lead the brotherhood, or that the Order is dependent upon him. Why then should he

leave instructions in any matter concerning the Order? . . .
Therefore, O Ananda, be ye lamps unto yourselves. Be ye
a refuge to yourselves.' (*Dialogues of the Buddha*, Part II,
pp. 107, 108. *See also The Book of the Kindred Sayings*,
Vol. V, p. 132.) Even earlier accounts also reveal Gotama's
disinterest in regulating conduct. For example, when some
mendicants wished to move to a western province to live,
they came to Gotama to seek permission. He asked them:
'Have you got leave, brethren, from the venerable Sariputta?' 'No, Master. . . .' 'Then do you get leave from . . .
Sariputta. He is the patron of those who live the righteous
life along with him.' (*The Book of the Kindred Sayings*, Vol.
III, p. 6.)

Dhamma (from Sanskrit *dharma*; established, firm,
steadfast; custom, practice, usage, decree, law, rules; according to the nature of anything) is another basic Buddhist
term having a long and devious history and embodying
great ambiguity. Gotama's *dhamma* as interpreted here
consists in his principle: to avoid frustration, stop desiring
what will not be attained (involving the middle way, i.e.,
by desiring neither more nor less than will be attained),
which has been stated as the four truths. But *dhamma*, in
the minds of some, has come to mean a special set of re-
strictive rules for monks. Between these two, and extending
beyond them, is a range of meanings something like the
following: *Dhamma* is any principle or law of nature,
whether of physical nature, moral nature, social nature, and
whether of universal or specific nature. *Dhamma* is, first,
Gotama's principle, and then his statement of it. As Gotama
became revered, worshipped, considered divine, *dhamma*
came to mean, first, statements made in explaining or
clarifying his principle, and then all his statements, without
exception. The *dhamma* became all statements attributed to

him, including some 'thus have I heard' statements of forgotten authorship. That trouble arose early regarding what
should be included in *dhamma* is evident from the following
which appeared in an early sutta, attributed to the Exalted
One: 'A brother may say thus, "From the mouth of the
Exalted One himself have I heard. . . . This is the truth, this
the teaching of the Master." The word spoken by that
brother should neither be received with praise nor treated
with scorn. . . . Every word and syllable should be carefully
understood and then put beside the Suttas (stock para-
graphs learnt by heart in the community) and compared
with the Vinaya (rules of the Order). If when so compared
they do not harmonize with the Suttas, and do not fit in with
the rules of the Order, then you may come to the conclusion: "Verily, this is not the word of the Exalted One,
and has been wrongly grasped by that brother. Therefore,
brethren, you should reject it." But if they harmonize . . . ,
then you may come to the conclusion: "Verily, this is the
word of the Exalted One." ' (*Dialogues of the Buddha*, Part
II, pp. 133–4.) *Dhamma* came to mean whatever was recorded in the Pitakas, first the Vinaya Pitaka and early
portions of the Sutta Pitaka, and then the later additions,
and finally the Abhidhamma Pitaka, first its early books,
then also its later books, and finally some of the commen-
taries upon them. Within Abhidamma other meanings
developed. For example, *dhammas* are 'the states of mental
and material existence'. (J. Kashyap, *The Abhidamma
Philosophy*, Vol. II, p. 32. Maha Bodhi Society, Sarnath,
Benares, India, 1943.)

'The rules of the Vinayapitaka were in point of fact
derived from various material sources, but on each law the
theory was superimposed that it has been promulgated
by Buddha on a certain occasion. To this theory all the

canonical writers are piously committed; it is in fact the setting in which nearly all Buddhist rules and doctrines are cast in early Pali literature. The consequence of the systematic application of this theory has been that the evolved character of the laws of the Vinayapitaka has been transparently veiled by an orthodox theory of their origin. Rules which are inconsistent with each other, and which clearly belong to different stages in the evolution of Buddhist monachism, are thus placed on the same chronological level by putting them into the mouth of Buddha. This Buddha, the promulgator of monastic laws, is not any historical personage, but only the embodiment of a theory representing the formal source of all Buddhist laws and doctrines.' (Sukumar Dutt, *Early Buddhist Monachism*, p. 28.) But 'both the rules of the Order, and the precepts laid down for laymen, are, from the Pitaka point of view, on a different plane altogether, lower than, apart from, that of the Path'. (T. W. Rhys Davids in *Dialogues of the Buddha*, Part I, p. 191.) 'When I am gone, Ananda, let the Order, if it should so wish, abolish all the lesser and minor precepts.' (*Dialogues of the Buddha*, Part II, p. 171.) 'Some foolish men master *dhamma*. . . . These, having mastered that *dhamma*, do not test the meaning of these things by intuitive wisdom; and these things whose meaning is untested by intuitive wisdom do not become clear. . . .' (*The Middle Length Sayings*, Vol I, p. 171.)

Why did Gotama, after advocating the middle way, remain a mendicant, a beggar? 'In those days the intellectual classes of India felt the ordinary activities of life to be unsatisfying; they thought it natural to renounce the world and mortify the flesh; divergent systems of ritual, theology and self-denial promised happiness but all agreed in thinking it normal as well as laudable that a man should devote his life to meditation and study. Compared with this frame of mind the teaching of the Buddha is not unsocial, unpractical and mysterious but human, business-like and clear. We are inclined to see in the monastic life which he recommended little but a useless sacrifice but it is evident that in the opinion of his contemporaries his disciples had an easy time, and that he had no intention of prescribing any cramped or unnatural existence.' (Charles Eliot, *Hinduism and Buddhism*, Vol. I, p. xx. Routledge and Kegan Paul, Ltd., London, 1921, 1954.)

Devotion to the higher things of life was an honoured way in his society (*see The Middle Length Sayings*, Vol. II, p. 304) and mendicancy as a necessary means to its pursuit was willingly supported under the customs of his day, as it is still in Burma, Ceylon, and Thailand, for example. When 'the parents of the boy Upali take counsel together, with regard to what they shall let the boy become, . . . they consider that he might get sore fingers from writing, or pains in his chest from arithmetic, or spoil his eyes with painting, and therefore determine to let him become a monk, because this is the most favourable way of earning a livelihood.' (Maurice Winternitz, *A History of Indian Literature*, Vol. II, pp. 29–30. Cf. *The Book of the Discipline*, Part IV, pp. 96–8.) Gotama was simply accepting things as they were in his society. Thirteen types of advantages of living the life of a recluse are discussed in the Samanna-Phala Sutta. (Cf. *Dialogues of the Buddha*, Part I, pp. 76–94.) When it was suggested that the reason Gotama 'frequents remote lodgings in forest and woodland wilderness' is that he was 'even today not devoid of attachment, not devoid of aversion, not devoid of confusion', he replied, 'But this is not to be taken in this way.' His purpose, rather, was to achieve 'for the self an abiding ease here and now. . . .' (*The Middle*

Length Sayings, Vol. I, p. 30.) 'The Bhikshu is satisfied with sufficient robes to cherish his body, with sufficient food to keep his stomach going. Whithersoever he may go forth, these things he takes with him as he goes—just as a bird with wings, whithersoever he may fly, carries his wings with him as he flies.' (*Dialogues of the Buddha*, Part I, p. 81.) Gotama was himself honoured as a great teacher; multitudes followed him, and many sought to wait on him, fan him, feed him, considering it an honour to do so. Despite his feeling a need for discounting honour ('I have naught to do with homage, Nagita, nor has homage aught to do with me.' (*The Book of the Gradual Sayings*, Vol. IV, p. 224)), his own circumstances appear to have been comfortable.

If it be noted that mendicancy involved abandonment of family and social responsibilities, it may be recalled that Jesus remained celibate and some Christian monks and priests must do likewise, and that, in Gotama's day, such abandonment required first fulfilling one's family and social obligations rather than escaping from them. Gotama first married and had a child; he left his family in good hands; he abandoned his rights to a kingdom as well as the responsibilities which went with them. When comparing mendicancy and householding, he asserted: 'My view is qualified, not absolute; I condemn wrong conduct alike in the (mendicant) and in the man with a house. With wrong conduct neither can attain to the true system or to the doctrine or to the right, but I commend right conduct in both alike: and with right conduct both alike can succeed.' Regarding mendicancy and business occupations, 'here again my view is qualified and not absolute. The busy life may be a failure and bear little fruit; or it may be a success and bear much fruit. So too the life without bustle may be either a failure or a success, bearing either little or much fruit. Take first the busy life. Agriculture however busily pursued may fail and bear little fruit; or again it may succeed and bear much fruit. On the other hand, commerce, if pursued without bustle, may either fail and bear little fruit; or again it may succeed and bear much fruit.' (*Further Dialogues of the Buddha*, Vol. II, pp. 113–14.)

Rules for monks, which abounded among the schools of thought in his day and since, were much discussed. But their mere instrumentality, or their irrelevency, was reiterated by Gotama again and again. After being told that it is not practice ('down to his being addicted to the practice of taking food, according to rule, at regular intervals . . .') but attitude which constitutes the middle way, Kassapa persists in inquiring about difficulties. Gotama continues: 'That is a common saying in the world that the life of a Samana and of a Brahmana is hard to lead. But if the hardness, the very great hardness, of that life depended merely on this asceticism, on the carrying out of any or all of those practices you have detailed, then it would not be fitting to say that the life of the Samana, of the Brahmana, was hard to lead. It would be quite possible for . . . any one . . . to say: "Let me now go naked . . .," and so on through all the items of those three lists of yours. But since, Kassapa, quite apart from these matters, quite apart from all kinds of penance, the life is hard, very hard to lead; therefore it is fitting to say: "How hard must be Samanaship to gain, how hard must Brahmanaship be!" For from the time, O Kassapa, when a Bhikku has cultivated the heart of love that knows no anger, that knows no ill will—from the time when by the destruction of the deadly intoxications (lusts of the flesh, the lust after future life, and the defilements of delusion and ignorance), he dwells in that emancipation of heart, in that emancipation of mind, that is, free from those intoxications, and that he, while yet in this visible world, has come to realize and know from that time, O Kassapa, it is that the Bhikku is called a Samana, is called a Brahmana.' (*Dialogues of the Buddha*, Part I, pp. 232, 234.)

Ananda once inquired of the Exalted One, 'Lord, to what extent may the Order of monks, as they live, live comfortably?' 'When, Ananda, a monk has achieved virtue by self and is no importuner of another as to more-virtue— to that extent, Ananda, may the Order, as they live, live comfortably.' 'But, lord, might there be another way where-in the Order, as they live, live comfortably?' 'There might be, Ananda. . . . When a monk . . . considers self and does not consider another—to that extent, Ananda, may the Order, as they live, live comfortably.' 'Lord, might there be yet another way . . .?' 'There might be. . . . When, thus having achieved . . , a monk is neither famous nor vexed by lack of fame—to that extent may the Order live comfort-ably.' 'Lord, might there be still another way . . . ?' 'There might. . . . When, so living . . . a monk obtains at will . . . the abodes of ease: the four jhanas . . . to that extent may the Order live comfortably.' 'Might there be some other way . . .?' 'There might. . . . Verily, Ananda, when a monk has achieved virtue by self, and is no importuner of another as to more-virtue; considers self, does not consider another; is neither famous nor vexed by lack of fame; obtains at will . . . the abodes of ease: the four jhanas . . .; and enters and abides in the emancipation of the mind, in the emancipation of insight . . . verily, Ananda, to that extent the Order of monks, as they live, may live comfortably. And I declare, Ananda, than this comfortable abode there is none higher, none loftier.' (*The Book of the Gradual Sayings*, Vol. III, pp. 102–3.)

Gotama's attitude toward the numerous rules guiding

monks and laymen throughout Buddhism's history should be clear. He was not interested in them except as means to the end. If the end can be approached directly, the means, the rules, are unnecessary. For those who cannot proceed directly, for those who need help, they may seek help anywhere they can find it. If by banding together and helping, encouraging, teaching, each other, men can make better progress, then they should do so. But they should do so only because this appears to them best suited to their needs, not because Gotama gave an authoritative command to do so. Many mendicants came to him for advice, and he advised them freely, always seeking to help them out of their particular predicament and, thereby, to reduce their anxiety. But many of the bits of advice he gave were remembered not as suggestions pertaining to peculiar circumstances but as everlasting rules without exceptions, and as mysteriously meritorious in themselves, while their original purpose of reducing anxiety directly is lost from sight.

Regarding food, for example, Gotama prescribed no special diet nor any hard and fast rules regarding how much or how little, or when and when not, or how or how not, to eat. But neither did he oppose those who did have definite ideas about these matters—so long as they were not conducive to anxiety. Indulging in an imaginative reconstruction of the spirit in which he taught about food, the writer suggests that Gotama accepted the common-sense conclusion that too little food leaves one weak and hungry, too much makes one bloated and dull, too spicy food overstimulates the appetite, while unpalatable food produces aversion. He had little reason to question the pattern of begging already established for himself and fellow mendicants. It is better to beg in the morning, when the temperature is cooler and the journey less exhausting, after a night's rest, and when one's appetite is ready for whatever is offered. In the morning, too, the people from whom one begs will have had a night's rest, will normally have prepared food for themselves after rising, and will have their own affairs less disturbed if monks come regularly at a time when they have left-over food. It is better to eat such food in the morning, for if kept through the heat of the day it is apt to spoil and attracts insects. In the evening people are more likely to be tired, more fearful of having outsiders approach after dark; there are more possibilities regarding temptations of various sorts; and it is more dangerous to come home in the dark. Popular experience with greedy monks, with the annoyance of having monks come too often, or stay too late, led naturally to certain general recommendations. The record itself has the monk Udayin explain why he thinks certain times for begging food are unadvisable: 'Once upon a time . . . when the monks were walking for almsfood in the dense darkness of the night, they would walk into a pool at the entrance to a village, and they would fall into the dirty pool near the village, and they would blunder into a thorny hedge, and they would blunder into a sleeping cow, and they would meet with young men, both those who had committed a crime and those who had not, and women would solicit them against true *dhamma*. Once upon a time I . . . used to walk for almsfood in the dense darkness of the night, and a certain woman saw me during a lightning flash as she was washing a bowl, and terrified at seeing me, she uttered a scream of horror: "How terrible for me, indeed there is a demon after me." . . . I . . . said to this woman: "Sister, I am not a demon, I am a monk standing for almsfood." She said: "The monk's father must be dead, the monk's mother must be dead—it were better for you, monk, to have your belly cut out with a sharp butcher's knife than to walk for almsfood for the sake of your belly in the dense darkness of the night." ' (*The Middle Length Sayings*, Vol. II, pp. 120–1. Tr. I. B. Horner, Luzac and Co., Ltd., London, 1957.)

What about killing animals for food? 'I hear it being said that people slay animals expressly for the recluse Gotama, who wittingly eats meat expressly meant for him and deliberately provided for him.' Is this correct? Not quite. Gotama advised against 'the eating of meat in three cases—if there is evidence either of your eyes or your ears or if there are grounds of suspicion. And in three cases I allow it—if there is no evidence of your eyes or of your ears and if there are no grounds for suspicion. Take the case of an almsman . . . to (whom) comes a householder . . . with an invitation to tomorrow's meal. If he so desires, the almsman accepts, and next morning . . . is served with an excellent meal. No thought comes to him that he could have wished his host either to desist now, or to desist in the future, from furnishing so excellent a meal; he eats his food without greed or blind desire but with a full consciousness of the dangers it involves and with full knowledge that it affords no refuge. Do you think that at such a time an almsman's thoughts are set on hurting himself, or others, or both?' 'No, sir.' 'Is not that almsman then eating food to which no blame attaches?' 'Yes, sir.' (*Further Dialogues of the Buddha*, Vol. I, p. 265.) Battling with an animal victim intended for food, especially if accompanied by an attitude of fear, hatred, brutality, or even of pity, is not conducive to calmness. In seeking calmness one should avoid such killing. However, also killing animals for food is a custom. One who follows the middle way is neither attached to nor repulsed by customs, is unanxious about any custom. It is also a custom to believe that killing of animals is an evil. If this is paradoxical, then it is a customary paradox, and one with which those who are willing to accept things as they are must be prepared to live. One may wish to stop the killing of animals, but if this desire grows into desirousness, generates restlessness, wilfulness, regarding interfering with the lives of others, then this desire to stop the killing of animals has become evil.

What about the yellow robe? Gotama prescribed no uniform for monks. He was against nakedness (Cf. *The Book of the Discipline*, Part IV, p. 4), but he did not say that one should never be naked. As representing austerity nakedness is one-sided and ineffective and as social it is distractive and disruptive. The wearing of clothes is simply better, to protect one from the sun, the wind, and insects. But one should not seek fine clothes, which stimulate pride in oneself, envy in others, and concern about soiling or spoiling or stealing. Why a robe? Was this typical of his time and culture—a style still reflected in women's saris? Why yellow? Surely Gotama was no more attached to one colour than another. Perhaps the colour was already established for mendicants before his time. The colour is reflected still in the robes worn today by Hindu swamis. A uniform colour is convenient both for those who feed the monks, so they can distinguish easily one kind of beggar from another, saintly devotee from lazy pauper, and for the monks who are thereby introduced with a minimum of disturbance. A uniform colour, like any symbol of occupation or profession, smooths the way. Uniformity of colour promotes indifference regarding colours which can be stimulating, distracting, and conducive to pride and envy.

What about medicines? Since Gotama's principle is psychological only, there is a temptation to think that he treated all healing as mental, or that one can be happy in spite of physical illness: 'Though my body is sick, my mind shall not be sick.' (*The Book of the Kindred Sayings*, Vol. III, p. 2.) But physical health and use of medicines should be dealt with in a common-sense manner. 'Wisely reflective, he uses the requisite medicines for the sick for warding off injurious feelings that have arisen, for the maximum of well-being. Whereas, monks, if he did not use (the requisites), the cankers which are destructive and consuming might arise, but because he does use (them), therefore these cankers which are destructive and consuming are not.' (*The Middle Length Sayings*, Vol. I, pp. 13–14.) Gotama not only approved medicines but he was willing that they be used whenever they were wanted. On one occasion, when monks were afflicted with an autumn disease causing them to be lean, yellowish, wretched, he gave a 'reasoned talk', saying: 'I allow you, monks, having accepted these five medicines (ghee, butter, oil, honey, molasses), to make use of them both at the right time and also at the wrong time.' (*The Book of the Discipline*, Part IV, p. 270.)

Was his advice only for monks and on monkly subjects? No. He advised all who came and on whatever problem was troubling them. All were in some sort of anguish and needed some restoration of common sense. Regarding caste duties, for example, he said: 'For myself, I neither assert that all service is to be rendered nor that all service is to be refused. If the service makes a man bad and not good, it should not be rendered; but if it makes him better and not bad, then it should be rendered. This is the guiding consideration which should decide the conduct alike of nobles, brahmins, of middle-class men and peasants.' (*Further Dialogues of the Buddha*, Vol. II, p. 101.) 'Whosoever are in bondage to the notions of birth or lineage, or to the pride of social position, or of connection by marriage, they are far from the best wisdom and righteousness. It is only by having got rid of all such bondage that one can realize for himself that supreme perfection in wisdom and in conduct.' (*Dialogues of the Buddha*, Part I, p. 123.) Gotama was not a zealous social reformer who struggled vigorously to tear down a vicious caste system, as some seem to believe. It is true that those who followed his middle way would automatically lose interest in supporting such a system, but it also is true that they would lose interest in destroying it. (*See The Middle Length Sayings*, Vol. II, pp. 273–8, 340–9, 366–71.)

Concerning government he made no significant remarks. The principle, accept things as they are, adequately interpreted, is conducive neither to conservatism nor to radicalism but to adaptationism, for things 'as they are' or 'are going to be' refers to opportunities for change as well as for remaining the same. The individual, to remain calm, should be willing to accept change when it comes and stability when it remains. Regarding complex modern political problems which were not prevalent in his day one can only infer that any form of government which arouses passion, animosity, eagerness, or ambition, or any other craving likely to lead to frustration, is to be avoided. Since war and politics are not conducive to calmness, they should be avoided as much as possible. Gotama's own example, abandoning a kingdom in search of enlightenment, may be taken as significant. He was not an anarchist. He did not oppose government. He was against anguish, and would have said that government governs best which governs with the least anxiety. His advice to the Vajjians illustrated his view: 'So long as the Vajjians shall be often assembled, much in assembly, growth for the Vajjians may be expected, not decline; so long as they shall sit down in concord, rise up in concord, do business in concord, growth may be expected, not decline; so long as they shall not decree the undecreed nor repeal the decreed, . . . growth may be expected . . .; so long as they shall not forcibly kidnap and make live with them women and girls of their own clan, growth may be expected. . . .' (*The Book of the Gradual Sayings*, Vol. IV, p. 10.)

Gotama was an atheist in the sense that he opposed attachment to any belief in god. Yet also he was opposed to attachment to any disbelief in god, because he was opposed to all frustrating attachment. If there are gods, and you desire what you get, or if there are no gods, and you desire what you get, the result is the same: you get what you desire. If there are gods, and you desire what will not be attained, or if there are no gods, and you desire what will not be attained, the result is the same: frustration. Hence the question, Is there or is there not a god? is an insignificant question. If people commonly believe in gods, and if such belief is inherent in one's culture, language, and inherited thought patterns, would it not be frustrating to try to dispute and disprove the existence of gods? 'Now, are there gods?' 'I knew offhand there were gods.' 'Why do you give that answer to my question, Gotama? Is it not false and untrue?' 'Anyone who, when asked if gods there be, answers that there are gods and he knew offhand there were —why, anyone of intelligence must come irresistibly to the conclusion that there are gods.' 'Why did you not make this clear at the outset, Gotama?' 'The world is loud in agreement that there are gods.' (*Further Dialogues of the Buddha*, Vol. II, pp. 122–3.) Furthermore, since, if there are gods, and any of them desire what they will not attain, they too will be frustrated, Gotama's principle applies to the gods also—in this or in other worlds, if such there be, as well as to animals and men. His principle is so fundamental and so universal that anyone concerned about lesser problems, such as is there or is there not a god, is being misled from a happy into an unhappy state.

Was Gotama a missionary? Although he lived and taught for forty-five years after his enlightenment, supposedly gathering multitudes of followers and establishing an order of teaching monks, he was not a missionary in the sense that he taught with eagerness or avidity for making converts. He was willing, but not wilful, to teach others (a trait still observable in Burmese bhikkus). Among his admirers were those who wondered why he was not more persistent in his teaching. When asked 'why sometimes it occurs to the tathagata to teach *dhamma* and sometimes it does not?' he replied, after listing cases where he did not, 'but when a monk . . . sits down to listen, questions the tathagata, listens with attentive ear, bears what he has heard in mind, tests the truth of the doctrines heard, . . . then it most occurs to the tathagata to preach *dhamma*'. (*The Book of the Gradual Sayings*, Vol. IV, pp. 220–1.) 'Just in the same way (as one who does not follow directions given him for getting to a town), brahmin, while *nirvana* exists and the road to it exists and I tell them the way, some of my disciples do and others do not succeed with this guidance and instruction. Where is my responsibility, brahmin? The truth-finder only indicates the way.' (*Further Dialogues of the Buddha*, Vol. II, p. 158.)

Was Gotama compassionate? Yes—as any man is compassionate in the presence of friends and of those in need. After his enlightenment, he sought out his previous way-faring companions who had struggled so diligently with him to find the way and he told them the good news. He was interested in their welfare. To all who came to him in earnest asking for help with their problems he was compassionate. But did he therefore uphold compassionateness as an ideal? No. The view that, upon achieving enlightenment, he did knowingly and unselfishly forgo immediate absorption into *nirvana* as complete desirelessness out of compassion for mankind is mistaken. And the Mahayanic view that Gotama conceived himself as a cosmic power for salvation which will not rest until every soul is saved from the evils of desire is also mistaken—so far as attributing this doctrine to Gotama as revealed in the Pitakas is concerned. Gotama's own view is that compassion, to the extent that it involves passion, zeal, anxiety, desirousness, longing, is to be avoided, though one ought not to wish for more stopping of compassionate interests than is in store for him. Too many interpreters of Gotama's philosophy overlook the fact that the middle way applies to compassionateness also. One should seek to be neither more compassionate nor less compassionate than he is going to be in the various circumstances in which he will find himself. As an ideal, compassionateness is definitely subordinated to the ideal of middle-wayedness.

He was not anxious about his reputation as a teacher. When two outsiders disputed, one condemning and one praising him, Gotama spoke thus to his followers: 'If outsiders should speak against me . . . you should not on that account either bear malice, or suffer heart-burning, or feel ill-will. If you, on that account, should be angry and hurt, that would stand in the way of your own self-conquest. If, when others speak against us, you feel angry at that, and displeased, would you then be able to judge how far that speech of theirs is well said or ill?' 'That would not be so, sir.' 'But when outsiders speak in dispraise of me . . . , you should unravel what is false and point it out as wrong, saying: "For this or that reason this is not the fact, that is not so, such a thing is not found among us, is not in us." But also, brethren, if outsiders should speak in praise of me . . . , you should not, on that account, be filled with pleasure or gladness, or be lifted up in heart. Were you to be so, that also would stand in the way of your self-conquest. When outsiders speak in praise of me . . . , you should acknowledge what is right to be the fact, saying: "For this or that reason this is the fact, that is so, such a thing is found among us, is in us." ' (*Dialogues of the Buddha*, Part I, pp. 2–3.)

12

CRITICISMS

EVEN though the philosophy of Gotama convincingly appeals to our common sense when it states a fundamental principle of human nature, it remains inadequate in certain respects. To the writer, who also advocates the ultimacy of middle-wayedness, Gotama's philosophy seems still one-sided in some ways. It appears to involve an imbalanced committment to the balanced way. His deliberate aloofness from either side of a controversy ('I quarrel not with the world. It is the world that quarrels with me. No preacher of the *dhamma* quarrels with anyone in the world. That which is not upheld in the world of the sages, that I declare, "It is not." What is upheld in the world of the sages, that I declare, "It is so." ' (*The Book of the Kindred Sayings*, Vol. III, p. 117.)) appears to commit him to one side of the aloofness versus non-aloofness controversy. His doctrine, at least, seems to praise serenity not moderately but extremely, even though accounts of his actual life indicate no aloofness from the problems which people brought to him. If, as appears from the record, he advocated persistent devotion to the middle way, did he not thereby abandon the middle way between persistent and non-persistent devotion to the middle way? Was he not too much attached to non-attachment and too much committed to non-commitment? Although any seeming lack of dialectical subtlety may be due to failure of reciters to convey it, must we not criticize Gotama's doctrine as inadequate to the extent that it fails to point to a middle way between the middle way and its opposites?

Gotama's philosophy appears inadequate also in that it consists in a single ultimate principle. Although this principle is philosophical in the sense that it holds true for all men at all times, yet his philosophy is inadequate to the extent that it fails to state all of the principles which hold true at all times. Gotama's principle is necessary to, but not sufficient for, an adequate philosophy of life. He expressed unusual wisdom in warning against 'greed for views' and, further, against 'greed for no views'. Yet the apparently deliberate neglect to seek metaphysical, epistemological, axiological, logical and other ultimate principles (a neglect doubtless much more warranted in his day than in ours) seems exceedingly close to 'greed for no views'. Thus there appears to be some justification for the claims of the various schools of Buddhism, and of rejectors of Buddhism, when they insist that, if he is to be accepted as a satisfactory guide, he should have made certain further assertions.

Four interrelated criticisms will be considered. Gotama's philosophy, as interpreted here, is not sufficiently realistic, not sufficiently voluntaristic, not sufficiently idealistic, and not sufficiently instrumentalistic.

Gotama was not sufficiently realistic. He was realistic in the sense that he recognized and accepted the existence of real things—things which exist independently of our knowing them. Real things contribute to our unhappiness when they stimulate desires which will not be satisfied. From these he advised aloofness. But his principle, being psychological only, neglected to emphasize the fact that real things may also contribute to our happiness when they satisfy our desires. Of course, when desires are satisfied, no problem exists; hence there seems to be no harm in neglecting them. But, many think, and not incorrectly, that if some things satisfy our desires and if more such things bring more satisfaction of desire, then in seeking more satisfaction, we ought to seek more such things. Thus a genuine problem, and one also crucially related to happiness, does exist. To the extent that happiness depends upon real things which satisfy desires, all of those principles related to the nature of real things conditioning their availability relative to such satisfactions are related to happiness. To the extent that Gotama conceived the principle of happiness to be psychological only, he failed to pursue a middle way between the psychological and the real.

Gotama was not sufficiently voluntaristic. He was voluntaristic in the sense that he recognized and accepted happiness as consisting in the satisfaction of desire, unhappiness as frustration of desire, and the problem of frustration of desire as life's most crucial problem. In this sense, he was completely voluntaristic. But apparently he neglected to stress positive assertions about the positive side of desire. (1) If there were no desire, there would be no satisfaction, hence no happiness; therefore happiness depends on desire. If happiness consists in the satisfaction of desire, then the more satisfaction, the more happiness. Hence, so long as the desires are satisfied, the more desires, the more satisfaction, and the more happiness. (2) Desire inspires, vitalizes, activates self. If there is no activity, there is no actor, no agent. Desire which stirs us to action makes us agents, initiators, powers. Desire creates self, if not entirely, then at least by instilling vitality, by bringing it to life. To be without desire is to be dead. To live is to desire and to desire is to live.

(3) Desire is enjoyable in itself, even if it ends eventually in frustration. The feeling of vitality is both an interesting and satisfying feeling. Desire not only gives life, but gives life its significance. Desire involves something desired, something desirable, something valued, something valuable. Desire begets value. And the greater the desire the greater the value. Hence, in a sense, intense desire, or desirousness, entails greater value than weak or calm desire. *Bhakti*, devotion, is also fundamental to happy living. (4) Desires often, if not always, entail some degree of anticipatory satisfaction. Unless one desires without knowing what he desires, how he pictures what he desires has some sense of satisfaction already inherent in his picture. Anticipatory satisfactions often are greater, richer, more enduring than the actual satisfaction itself. Anticipatory satisfaction is value enjoyed, even for those desires eventually frustrated. (5) Desire may have utility, in the sense that it may stimulate still other desires, and in so far as such desire begets value it thereby stimulates the begetting of still other values. Desire may have utility also in that it may induce effort to achieve goods, whether by changing the world or by changing oneself. William James' discussions of the will-to-believe provide illustrations of values produced by willing, or in which willing itself is the decisive factor in achieving value. Sometimes one must desire more than he is going to get of some things (i.e., be willing to risk, even expect, frustration, as in trial and error learning) in order to get as much as he wants of certain other things (e.g., skill in satisfying desires persistently and efficiently). This brings us to the problem of choice.

(6) Desire is the basis of choice. If no desire, then no desire to choose among desirables, and no choice. If no choice, then no choosing among alternatives, no evaluation,

no principle for evaluation, and no ethics. But actually men constantly are faced with choosing between alternatives, not merely the alternatives of accepting or not accepting things as they are, but also other alternatives between good and bad, better and worse, greater and lesser values. Another fundamental ethical principle, 'When faced with alternatives, always choose the greater good', is missing from Gotama's *dhamma*. Although he actually employed it, both in giving advice on varieties of matters concerning which he was consulted and in defending his own principle that *nirvana* as middle-wayedness is the greatest good, he failed to formulate and assert it. But this principle is just as fundamental as his. So his omission may be considered evidence that he gave inadequate attention to the positive values of desire.

(7) Desire is a basis of freedom—not of freedom from desire but of freedom to desire, and of freedom to choose. No freedom of choice can exist without desire. Surely freedom of choice is a fundamental positive value. Such freedom depends upon both objective opportunities and subjective capacities, including the willingness to choose. One does not need to go to such extremes as those existentialists who claim that authentic life has both its beginning and ending in choosing, especially in anxious if futile conflict of choices, in order to recognize that the act of choosing, deciding, determining, entails appreciable vitality and significance. To choose to be choiceless is almost on a par with suicide. Gotama did not advocate complete choicelessness, but only relaxed choosing. Yet apparently he did not explicitly advocate freedom of choice as being equally fundamental with being relaxed.

Now it is true that, if all of the foregoing seven items refer to parts of things as they are, Gotama, in advocating acceptance of things as they are, advocated, by implication, accepting all these things. Hence to criticize him for being not sufficiently voluntaristic is, in this sense, unfair. Yet to the extent that there are many equally fundamental principles pertaining to things as they are, to point out that he intended to emphasize only one as fundamental, if he did so intend, is not unfair. There is a middle way between emphasizing only one as most fundamental and emphasizing all as equally fundamental which Gotama appears to have neglected.

Gotama was not sufficiently idealistic. Relative to the distinction between the actual and the ideal, he idealized acceptance of the actual rather than attachment to ideals (even though, in this actually unhappy world, his principle for removing unhappiness, i.e., accept the actual, remains an ideal). Granted that many idealists have been extremists, subordinating the actual to the ideal, nevertheless when the ideal collapses into the actual, something essential to human happiness is missing. 'Our reach exceeds our grasp, or what's a heaven for?' Gotama's dialectical acceptance of ideals as part of things as they are does not excuse neglect to state that they are just as ultimate as his principle. Of course, one must accept things as they are, and such possibilities of and opportunities for improvement as there are; but to the extent that such possibilities and opportunities are genuine, failure to recognize them to be such is a failure to recognize things as they are. If the future is partly open, and progress is possible, and attachment to ideals provides power to change things for the better, failure to accept the challenge to help change things for the better is to fail to accept such actual challenge as part of what is. Although too many are too idealistic, wasting their lives pursuing unrealizable ideals, nevertheless one may be too actualistic, destroying possibilities for future happiness by refusing to have any interest in future life. Gotama advocated extreme actualism. Yet actually, also, he was a great idealist in hoping that many more would pursue the middle way (i.e., cease to be idealists). But to the extent that he failed to advocate a middle way between actualism and idealism, his *dhamma* was not sufficiently idealistic and not sufficiently middle-wayed.

Gotama was not sufficiently instrumentalistic. Relative to the distinction between means and end or way and goal, his *dhamma* stressed attention to the end or goal rather than to the means, the way, as instrumental to the goal. Now it is true that the end is prior to the means, and there can be no way to a goal without a goal. Also, if the goal is intrinsic value and the way is instrumental value, it is foolish to waste needless effort upon the instrumental if this subtracts from enjoyment of the intrinsic. If *nirvana* is at hand, in this very life, in this very moment, why sacrifice sure enjoyment of *nirvana* for anxious efforts regarding an uncertain to-morrow? Gotama was most wise in insisting upon these facts. However, the import of all this is that the means should be telescoped into the end as much as possible. *Nirvana*, traditionally, connotes end completely freed from means. But actually means and end are mutually dependent, all ends being ends of means as well as means being means to ends. Actually this very moment is experienced both as being what it is and as leading toward the future, and such leading constitutes the means-character of experience. Granted that there is a fundamental sense in which the way is the goal and the goal is the way, such way-goal remains both way and goal; and wayfulness or instrumentality is as essential to it as goalness or terminality; hence attention to instrumentality is equally essential.

Of course, instrumentalism may also be carried to extremes, as by John Dewey, who at times appears to claim that only means are important since, for him, no intrinsic values exist. The writer stands between, or pursues a middle path between, Dewey's extreme instrumentalism and Gotama's extreme terminalism. Gotama, in accepting things as they are, was willing to accept this middle way. Yet the record fails to reveal that he advocated more than permissive interest in means. Active interest in means aims to bring us to our goal more quickly. Also, what appears to be merely a means often turns out unexpectedly to be an end (cf. hedonistic paradox); for the goal is to be found in the way, even when we are not looking for it. If, or to the extent that, the way is the goal and the goal is the way, the pursuer of the way, the instrumentalist, may thereby be enjoying the goal even though he does not recognize that he is doing so. Gotama himself was advocating his *dhamma* as the way or means to *nirvana*, even though his *dhamma* itself advocated emphasis on the end rather than the means. Hence this criticism is directed not so much at Gotama's actual behaviour as at a degree of inadequacy in his doctrine.

Some critics may wish to claim that the writer has set up a straw man, or straw *dhamma*, first claiming that the eightfold path was intended not as step-wise (instrumental) but as illustrative aspects or areas of *nirvana* (terminal), and then condemning Gotama for being insufficiently instrumentalistic. Such criticism would have point only if, or to the extent that, step-wise procedure was intended by Gotama. Yet even if step-wise prodecure were intended relative to those eight folds, the whole emphasis of Gotama's *dhamma* centres in the view that means exist for the sake of end, whereas the writer more middle-wayedly claims that means and end exist for, by, and through each other. The mutual dependence of means and end upon each other entails a double priority; end is prior to means and also means is prior to end, each, means and end, having its own kind of priority, and each kind of priority being equally ultimate. To the extent that the writer follows Gotama's *dhamma*, he must be willing to accept things as they are, including Gotama's *dhamma* as it is, his own inadequacies as an interpreter for what they are and the criticisms of all critics for whatever they turn out to be. But in doing so he also accepts a middle path between accepting things as they are and not accepting things as they are as, dialectically, part of things as they actually are. Whatever this study may lead to (instrumentally), it, including its interpretation or misinterpretation, has been enjoyed also as an end-in-itself. Anxiety has existed regarding whether or not it could be brought to satisfactory conclusion; but at the same time sufficient confidence (*nirvana*) has also prevailed, and been enjoyed, to enable reaching such conclusion. Note, here, that such confidence (*nirvana*, end) served as a means useful for finishing this instrument.

To the four foregoing criticisms, others pertaining to insufficient compassionateness, insufficient interest in political and social and economic affairs, insufficient interest in logic, etc., might be added. Yet all of these criticisms, it should be remembered, are not so much criticisms of Gotama the man in his own cultural context as they are criticisms of those who would have us accept his *dhamma* as sufficient for today, after two and a half millennia of *dhammic* development. Of course, criticisms of this type, implying that he should have stated all of the universal truths and that he should have known and said more than he did, are unfair, and represent an unwillingness to accept him for what he was. On the other hand, such criticisms surely would not have been motivated in the first place were it not for the fact that some of his worshippers have claimed for him impossible types of omniscience, thereby not accepting him for what he was but unfairly demanding that he be more than he had been. One unfairness begets another, but does not justify it. Only when one is willing to accept such unfairness as there is as part of things as they are is he willing to be fair even to the unfair. Gotama, it must be said, had such willingness.

Perhaps it is appropriate to append some remarks about other philosophies also appearing in the Pitakas. That Theravada doctrines are to be found in them is not questioned. Inquiry into how many and what other philosophies are expressed has not been attempted. But the effort to extract what seems to be Gotama's own philosophy from the various views has required some speculation regarding which suttas more nearly express Gotama's teachings and which do not. The following hypothesis is suggested, not as conclusive, but for the purpose of stimulating further consideration.

That each of Gotama's fellow-questers had his own ideals, some closer to, some more divergent from, those of Gotama is clear. But how much each disciple, or partial disciple, modified Gotama's teaching in the retelling, innocently or deliberately, is not so clear. Yet it may well be that Gotama's own philosophy can be reconstructed adequately only after first determining what type of refraction was likely to occur in the different mental prisms of each of his various reporters. The writer ventures to predict that some such study will be made eventually and with partial success.

On the positive side, those suttas which have a common-sense, down-to-earth, obvious character about them, those in which some simple problem is dealt with intelligently (*vs.* didactically), those in which Gotama is addressed as Gotama or as Tathagata (*vs.* as Exalted One), seem more likely to reflect an original message. If the writer's thesis is correct, then those expressing a spirit of relaxation, of accepting things as they are, especially those making the middle way appear clear and reasonable, probably more genuinely convey Gotama's own intentions.

On the negative side, characteristics appearing likely to indicate distortion of clear mirroring of Gotama's *dhamma* may be grouped into five overlapping groups, pertaining to believers, worshippers, monks, transmitters, and compilers.

If Gotama, following his middle way between belief and disbelief, expressed no opinion regarding issues, then those suttas in which opinion is expressed regarding such issues appear to be influenced by other minds. Thus, for example, those in which *karma*, rebirth, the no-soul doctrine and what is implied by the no-soul doctrine (e.g., *skandhas* and related details of physiology, breathing, and control of attention) were advocated, and those involving cosmological interpretations of the *jhanas*, as well as those claiming certain things to be impossible, violate the spirit of the middle way. Gotama was neither, strictly, a Theravadin nor a Mahayanist.

Worshippers, by attaching special reverence to Gotama (especially in competition with other gods, including Mara), tend to attribute to Gotama miraculous powers far beyond those intended by him (e.g., travelling or stretching an arm great distances instantaneously, recalling feats in previous lives, manifesting detailed omniscience or cosmic compassionateness). Poetical suttas, expressing reverence for or attachment to Gotama rather than Gotama's attitude of appreciative indifference, i.e., neither worshipping nor not worshipping, appear to be the work of modifiers. (*See also* C. A. F. Rhys Davids, *Minor Anthologies of the Pali Canon*, Vol. I, pp. xxviii–xxix, Oxford University Press, London, 1931.)

Suttas expressing grave concern for details of monkish rules, especially those devoted to justifying the rules and those pertaining to expulsions from the order, reflect the interests of reporters deeply involved in an organized monastic society. Gotama, while not unacquainted with efforts of monks to regulate self-discipline in themselves and followers, was probably not positively interested in, even if acquainted with, the *Patimokkha*.

Transmitters, especially memorizers, developed vested interests in mnemonic devices which led them to give emphasis and special significance to enumeration as enumeration and formula as formula. Suttas in which there is little or no live dialogue (Gotama was an exciting conversationalist), expressing regular and complete repetition of formal detail more than vital, free-flowing argument, probably becloud original intent. Not only formal, but seeming, after multitudinous repetitions, extremely artificial, the 'thus have I heard' beginings and 'thus spake the lord' endings of suttas appear to express complete absence of originality.

Suttas which are obviously composite, especially when their parts appear elsewhere in more lively form and when long lists of doctrinal summaries fit awkwardly together, reflect the handiwork of minds with different interests. Gotama, being devoted to a single fundamental principle, was not attached to system or to systematizing. Suttas too long for a single conversation, or for remembering such a conversation, must have been compiled. Hence extremely long suttas (as well as extremely short ones—formalized fragments of a problematic situation) probably imply distance from the source. Finally, those suttas in which the only auditor is reported as killed immediately after the discourse (Cf. *Further Dialogues of the Buddha*, Vol. II, pp. 290–5) must give rise to some doubt.

The foregoing proposals, which are entirely negative in the sense that they suggest which suttas do not best represent the philosophy of Gotama, need to be supplemented by positive hypotheses as to which of the reported disciples, Ananda, Sariputta, Kassapa, etc., were most influential in presenting those other philosophies which are also clearly expressed in the Pitakas. (*See* C. A. F. Rhys Davids, *Gotama, the Man*, especially Ch. VI and pp. 33, 52, 72f., 76f., 122f., 138f., 158f., 180f., 190f., 197, 209f., 215, 220f., 242. Luzac and Co., Ltd., London, 1928.)

This book is finished, but its work is not done. Despite the persistence with which its thesis has been expressed, it remains intended as tentative, and as provocative of more research into the nature and purposes of the Pitakas. Growing interest of the world in Buddhism and of Buddhists in critical scholarship converge in the founding of the new International Institute for Advanced Buddhistic Studies in Rangoon concurrently with the two-year celebration by the Sixth World Council of Buddhists, marking two and a half millennia of Buddhist history. The founding of this Institute offers great hope.

BIBLIOGRAPHY

The Book of the Discipline (Vinaya Pitaka), Part I (Suttavibhanga), tr. I. B. Horner, Oxford University Press, London, 1938.

The Book of the Discipline, Part II (Suttavibhanga), tr. I. B. Horner, Oxford University Press, London, 1940.

The Book of the Discipline, Part III (Suttavibhanga), tr. I. B. Horner, Oxford University Press, London, 1942.

The Book of the Discipline, Part IV (Mahavagga), tr. I. B. Horner, Luzac and Co., Ltd., London, 1951.

The Book of the Discipline, Part V (Cullavagga), tr. I. B. Horner, Luzac and Co., Ltd., London, 1952.

The Book of the Gradual Sayings (Anguttara Nikaya), Vol. I, tr. F. L. Woodward, Luzac and Co., Ltd., London, 1932, 1951.

The Book of the Gradual Sayings, Vol. II, tr. F. L. Woodward, Luzac and Co., Ltd., London, 1933, 1951, 1952.

The Book of the Gradual Sayings, Vol. III, tr. E. M. Hare, Luzac and Co., Ltd., London, 1934, 1952.

The Book of the Gradual Sayings, Vol. IV, tr. E. M. Hare, Luzac and Co., Ltd., London, 1935, 1955.

The Book of the Gradual Sayings, Vol. V, tr. F. L. Woodward, Luzac and Co., Ltd., London, 1936, 1955.

The Book of the Kindred Sayings (Samyutta Nikaya), Vol. I, tr. C. A. F. Rhys Davids, Luzac and Co., Ltd., London, 1917, 1950.

The Book of the Kindred Sayings, Vol. II, tr. C. A. F. Rhys Davids, Luzac and Co., Ltd., London, 1922, 1952.

The Book of the Kindred Sayings, Vol. III, tr. F. L. Woodward, Luzac and Co., Ltd., London, 1925, 1954.

The Book of the Kindred Sayings, Vol. IV, tr. F. L. Woodward, Luzac and Co., Ltd., London, 1927, 1956.

The Book of the Kindred Sayings, Vol. V, tr. F. L. Woodward, Luzac and Co., Ltd., London, 1930, 1956.

Dialogues of the Buddha (Digha Nikaya), Part I, tr. T. W. Rhys Davids, Oxford University Press, London, 1899, 1923.

Dialogues of the Buddha, Part II, tr. T. W. and C. A. F. Rhys Davids, Oxford University Press, London, 1910, Luzac and Co., Ltd., London, 1919, 1951.

Dialogues of the Buddha, Part III, tr. T. W. and C. A. F. Rhys Davids, Oxford University Press, London, 1921.

Further Dialogues of the Buddha (Majjhima Nikaya), Vol. I, tr. Lord Chalmers, Oxford University Press, London, 1926.

Further Dialogues of the Buddha, Vol. II, tr. Lord Chalmers, Oxford University Press, London, 1927.

The Middle Length Sayings (Majjhima Nikaya), Vol. I, tr. I. B. Horner, Luzac and Co., Ltd., London, 1954.

The Middle Length Sayings, Vol. II, tr. I. B. Horner, Luzac and Co., Ltd., London, 1957. (Vol. III was not available.)

The Minor Anthologies of the Pali Canon (Khuddaka Nikaya), Vol. I (Khuddaka-patha: The reading of small passages; and Dhammapada: Words of the Doctrine), tr. C. A. F. Rhys Davids, Oxford University Press, 1931.

The Minor Anthologies of the Pali Canon, Vol. II (Udana: Verses of Uplift; and Itivuttaka: As It Was Said), tr. F. L. Woodward, Oxford University Press, London, 1935, 1948.

The Minor Anthologies of the Pali Canon, Vol. III (Buddhavamsa: The lineage of the Buddhas; and Cariyapitaka: Collection of Ways of Conduct), tr. B. C. Law, Oxford University Press, London, 1938.

The Minor Anthologies of the Pali Canon, Vol. IV (Vimanavatthu: Stories of the Mansions; and Petavatthu: Stories of the Departed), tr. Jean Kennedy and H. S. Gehman, respectively, Luzac and Co., Ltd., London, 1942.

Psalms of the Early Buddhists, Vol. I. *Psalms of the Sisters* (Theri-Gatha), tr. C. A. F. Rhys Davids, Pali Text Society, London, 1909, 1949.

Psalms of the Early Buddhists, Vol. II. *Psalms of the Brethren* (Thera-Gatha), tr. C. A. F. Rhys Davids, Pali Text Society, London, 1913, 1937.

Woven Cadences of Early Buddhists (Suttanipata), tr. E. M. Hare, Oxford University Press, London, 1945, 1947.

(English translation of four other collections of suttas included in the Sutta Pitaka, i.e., of the *Jataka, Niddesa, Apadana*, and *Patisambhidha-magga*, were not used in this study.)

BURTT, E. A., *The Teachings of the Compassionate Buddha*, New American Library, New York, 1955.

CHATTERJEE, S. C., and DATTA, D. M., *An Introduction to Indian Philosophy*, University of Calcutta, 1939, 1954.

CONZE, EDWARD, *et al.*, *Buddhist Texts Through the Ages*, Philosophical Library, New York, 1954.

DUTT, N., *Aspects of Mahayana Buddhism in its Relation to Hinayana*, Luzac and Co., Ltd., London, 1930.

DUTT, SUKUMAR, *Early Buddhism Monachism*, Kegan Paul, Trench, Trubner and Co., Ltd., London, 1924.

ELLIOT, CHARLES, *Hinduism and Buddhism*, Vol. I, Routledge and Kegan Paul, Ltd., London, 1921, 1954.

HUMPHREYS, CHRISTMAS, *Buddhism*, Penguin Books, Harmondsworth, Middlesex, 1951.

JENNINGS, J. G., *The Vedantic Philosophy of the Buddha*, Oxford University Press, London, 1948.

KASHYAP, J., *The Abhidhamma Philosophy*, Two Vols., Maha-Bodhi Society, Sarnath, Benares, 1942, 1943.

KEITH, A. BERRIEDALE, *Buddhist Philosophy in India and Ceylon*, Oxford University Press, London, 1923.

MONIER-WILLIAMS, M., *A Sanskrit-English Dictionary*, Oxford University Press, London, 1899.

NARASU, P. LAKSHMI, *The Essence of Buddhism*, Thacker and Co., Ltd., Bombay, 1907, 1948.

RHYS DAVIDS, C. A. F., *Gotama, The Man*, Luzac and Co., Ltd., London, 1928.

RHYS DAVIDS, T. W., and STEDE, W., *Pali-English Dictionary*, Pali Text Society, London, 1925, 1949.

SINGH, MOHAN, *New Light on Buddha's First Sermon*, Academy of Spiritual Culture, Elephanta, Dhera Dun, 1949.

THOMAS, EDWARD J., *The Life of Buddha, As Legend and History*, Routledge and Kegan Paul, Ltd., London, 1927, 1949.

WINTERNITZ, MAURICE, *A History of Indian Literature*, Vol. II, University of Calcutta, 1933.

INDEX

CAPRICORN TITLES